MIND, MONEY, AND WEALTH

WHAT THEY DON'T TEACH IN SCHOOL

ROBERT LUXENBERG

LIONCREST
PUBLISHING

MIND, MONEY, AND WEALTH

What They Don't Teach in School

ISBN   978-1-5445-0164-2 *Paperback*

        978-1-5445-0163-5 *Ebook*

        978-1-5445-0293-9 *Audiobook*

This book is my legacy to you, Evan, Sarah, and Deanna. I love each of you very much. I am proud of the extraordinary individuals you are becoming.

As young adults, you are gaining excellent teachings and information from your schools. I have written this book to augment your learning with real-world wisdom about your mind and how it works, money and how it works, and how to build legacy wealth. None of these things are really taught properly in school, but they are essential to achieving the freedom you desire. Remember, the more money you make, the more freedom you have to live your dreams, and the more people you can help!

Daddy, I know you are watching my journey from above. I hope you are proud of your son and the choices I have made. This book is dedicated to your memory.

CONTENTS

INTRODUCTION

Here's a truth you won't learn in school: you don't need a high IQ or wealthy parents to be financially successful. In fact, you don't even need a college education. Many of the millionaires being made in North America every day did not graduate from university.

Schools are designed to train you for a job, but most educators are not equipped to teach you about entrepreneurship or how to build wealth. When you graduate, you might be ready for a career, but you likely haven't been taught how money really works.

Now, if your plan is to one day be a lawyer or a doctor, school is where you want to be. You'll need years of education and training, plus above-average grades to enter those fields. The requirements are rigorous, but if you jump through all the hoops, you'll be rewarded with a high salary, great benefits, and plenty of stability.

Congratulations! Your prestigious profession means you're now wealthy.

Or are you?

A lot of kids today, with some urging from their parents, dream of landing a high-paying job when they grow up because they want the luxuries that become possible when you're making a lot of money: the house with the in-ground pool and home movie theater, a couple of Mercedes or BMWs in the garage, and family vacations to Bali and Dubai.

Doctors, lawyers, and those in similarly high-paying positions are able to enjoy the perks that come with a nice income, giving them the outward appearance of wealth.

However, you shouldn't assume that means they're wealthy.

Some high-income individuals are wealthy because they've invested their money in assets like real estate that can provide a high return on investment (ROI).

But for many high-income individuals, if you took away

their paycheck, they'd be left with a shallow bank account and expensive luxuries they could no longer afford. Their income and possessions create the illusion of wealth, but in reality, they'd have no safety net to catch them if their ability to make money through their profession stopped tomorrow.

True wealth comes from what you do with your money, not how much of it you make.

TO BUILD WEALTH, START WHEN YOU'RE YOUNG

You can see why financial success is about more than a high IQ or years of education. Sure, you'll need basic financial knowledge, but it's more important to have the right mindset so you can create a plan and then act on it.

Intelligence doesn't hurt, but you'll be better served with the right mindset as well as certain skills and information generally not taught in school. You'll also need another type of intelligence: the ability to form relationships, connect with people, understand them, and then communicate to *get what you want!*

With these ingredients, you can become a millionaire or even a billionaire. What will help your chances is starting when you're young. The more years you have to work on building wealth, the wealthier you can become. Time is the ultimate X factor, but it can't be bought or sold. You have to use it while you have it or be prepared to work much harder later in life to make up for those years you didn't capitalize on your opportunity. This isn't to say you can't create wealth when you're older. I did it! There is no expiry date on success.

I couldn't fathom becoming a millionaire when I was young. I knew I had the skills and the brains to get there, but I had no idea how to make it happen. The more people I've spoken with about this topic, the more I realize how many people feel the same way I felt.

I can become a millionaire? Really?

You absolutely can. In fact, it can happen rather quickly. I know people who've followed the path laid out in this book and watched as their net worth soared past $100 million.

The difference between making $50,000 a year and $1 million a year is *awareness*.

Once you're aware of what's out there, understand how it works, and begin to take advantage of it, nothing can stop you from creating the life of your dreams.

WHY AREN'T MORE PEOPLE WEALTHY?

I'm not a mind reader, but I can guess what you're thinking: *This sounds too good to be true. If there's such a simple formula to building wealth, why aren't more people wealthy?*

There are several reasons why everyone isn't wealthy. It starts with a fact we discussed earlier: school doesn't teach you about money or how to build wealth. Teachers spend a lot of time on math, formulas, and theories, but they seem to miss the basics and what works in the *real* world. If you get a chance, you should watch a movie (available on Netflix) called *Back to School* with Rodney Dangerfield. Aside from the fact it is really funny (Rodney is my favorite comedian), there is an excellent scene where Rodney takes on the professor regarding textbook theories versus the real world. It encapsulates the problem quite well.

I saw the lack of key information in school when I asked my nineteen-year-old son, Evan, and his friends if they knew about compound interest. They had all received a top education from various private high schools in Montreal, yet they had no idea what I was talking about.

Albert Einstein once called compound interest the most powerful force in the universe, yet it's not taught in most high schools. If you want to learn about this powerful force that creates money like magic, you've come to the right place. We'll talk about it a lot in this book.

Compound interest is the eighth wonder of the world. He who understands it, earns it. He who doesn't, pays it.

ALBERT EINSTEIN

Schools also don't teach you about the incredible power of your mind. It's an instrument to be reckoned with. New curriculum in more proactive schools is starting to reflect the need for critical thinking, problem-solving, and mind-power, but it'll be another generation before we see the impact of those changes. Because they don't learn how to use their mind, many kids come out of school thinking they *are* their mind. As we'll see in the next few chapters, that's not true. Your mind is an instrument to be wielded and controlled as you see fit.

Students who come out of school with a limited mindset grow into adults who view wealth as unattainable. They see it like a golden ticket that only a lucky few ever receive.

When I told my mom I was a millionaire, she was flabbergasted. She simply couldn't wrap her mind around how I'd created so much wealth in such a short amount of time.

In fact, some in my family were convinced I'd started dealing drugs or something! Isn't that insane? My own family would sooner believe I'd resorted to a life of crime than believe I'd become a millionaire by following a simple wealth-building blueprint—no tricks or shortcuts, just the right mindset, the knowledge I needed, and a plan I executed with enthusiasm.

Fear also holds people back from becoming wealthy. We all deal with fear on a daily basis. The difference is that successful people like Warren Buffett, Elon Musk, and Michael Bloomberg know how to manage their fear. They still experience fear, but it doesn't slow them down.

MONEY MISCONCEPTIONS THAT LIMIT US

Misconceptions about money can also hold people back. Perhaps the most popular is that making lots of money is somehow based on the number of hours worked. People incorrectly assume that the more hours you put in and the harder you work, the more money you make. This is true to a certain extent, but what I want you to understand is that building wealth has little to do with the number of hours you work.

Truthfully, you're not wealthy until you're making money while you sleep.

Another misconception is that wealthy people pay significant taxes. Five years ago, I was in Fiji for a Tony Robbins seminar. The one hundred smart, successful people in the room with me were asked to raise their hand to indicate how much they paid in taxes the year before. As the moderator counted down from 50 percent, to 40 percent, then 30 percent, every hand went up but mine.

The facilitator noticed I just sat there without raising my hand and asked me how much I paid in taxes the previous year. I sheepishly explained that I hadn't paid any taxes. I'd made a lot of money, but the government hadn't gotten a dime, at least not in the short run.

Now, before you go calling the Canada Revenue Agency or the IRS on me, I wasn't admitting to tax evasion with my answer. It is incumbent on us as individuals to understand the tax code the best we possibly can and push it to the limit without crossing the line.

Those aren't my words. They're clearly written into the beginning of the tax code itself! And I followed the tax code verbatim.

Our government wants us to know the tax laws and do the best we can with them. I found a perfectly legal way to avoid paying taxes by deferring them to the future.

Yet if you tell someone you didn't pay taxes on the money you made last year, they'll likely think you're cheating the system. In reality, they're the ones being cheated, and all because they didn't take the time to learn more about advantages available through the tax laws.

MY FINANCIAL JOURNEY GOT STARTED LATE

I didn't discover the formula for building wealth until I was forty-seven years old. Yikes, I can't believe it took me until the age of forty-seven! I was an excellent student with an above-average IQ. I even had pretty good communications skills and a sharp mind. So why wasn't I successful and rich like I fully expected to be many years previously?

I spent my career staring at the formula without realizing what I was seeing. It wasn't until I was offered a position with a Montreal company to spearhead its efforts in the United States that I realized something was very wrong.

For many years, I'd worked hard in every position I held and earned a nice living. I overdelivered in every position and portfolio I took on. I had days as a real estate agent where I walked out of work with a $50,000 check.

When I was a corporate executive for certain companies, there were opportunities to benefit significantly, if only the CEOs made the right decisions or the circumstances were more favorable. During the dot-com boom, I was a vice president of a company that was ready to launch with a board of directors that most companies dream of. We had a valuation of $80 million, and I had 5 percent equity. It was a real chance to be a millionaire, or so I thought. Before we had a chance to launch and go public, the dot-com crash came. Our company went bankrupt and my millions disappeared.

I had a similar experience with another company, whose acquisition was dashed when the CEO couldn't close the deal. Again, millions disappeared.

Though I'd been working hard and making a living, after forty-seven years, I had nothing to show for it and I'd built zero wealth.

So, I returned home after being wined and dined by the CEO and other senior executives of the company I was about to work for, and I had a chest pain like you cannot imagine. I thought I was having a heart attack. What I realized was that my mind and body were sending me a strong and clear message.

Bob, you've been there and done that. The corporate route hasn't worked for you. You've tried it not once, not twice, but several times and never attained the results you hoped for. You've achieved no freedom. Are you really going to keep doing this?

Then, on the radio, the song "Cat's in the Cradle" by Harry Chapin began to play. It's the story of a father and son. The son asks the father to play ball with him, but the father is always too busy. In the second part of the song, the son is older now, and when his father asks to spend time with him, the son tells him he has no time: "We'll get together then. You know we'll have a good time then." Of course, they never did spend time together. *What you sow is what you reap*. Listening to this song and realizing that the job with this company entailed so much traveling and time away from my children, I began to cry. I saw I would have little time to play with my children, the loves of my life.

I was at a crossroads. I could make the safe choice and take the job. Or I could do something most people wouldn't do with three young kids at home and very little money in the bank: call the company and tell them I wasn't joining their team.

I chose the second option.

My first move after I called the CEO and broke the news (*note*: he didn't take it well) was to call Norm, an old client of mine. I'd sold Norm his first two buildings when I was working as a real estate agent. I found him to be highly analytical and very smart with money, so I asked him if he'd have breakfast with me so I could pick his brain.

When we got together, I told Norm my story and my pain— and that I turned down the job offer.

"Norm, you're a smart guy who became a millionaire in real estate," I said as we ate. "You've now heard my story. Tell me where I've gone wrong. What should I be doing?"

He looked at me and said, "Bob, this is not complicated. Number one, you've got to work for yourself. You can't work for other people, because all you're doing is making them rich, and you have no real control over your own destiny. Number two, do what you know best. All these years you helped people buy property and become wealthy, but you never did it yourself. You should get into real estate. You know it well."

Norm was right. Real estate was a great fit for me, but I wasn't prepared to tackle it alone. I needed some help. Although Norm was semiretired and spent his days playing bridge (he achieved Sapphire Life Master), his net worth was slowly dwindling. He wasn't looking for a new opportunity, but he needed one.

"Why don't you do this with me?" I asked him. "Let's buy some property together."

He thought about it and said, "You know what? That's a good idea."

That was the start of our partnership fourteen years ago. We built our business from scratch and have done quite well. Before I celebrated my fiftieth birthday, I became a millionaire, and soon after, a multimillionaire.

I never would've reached that milestone had I made the safe choice.

MINDSET AND KNOWLEDGE LAY THE FOUNDATION

In the first part of this book, we'll look at what it takes to develop a money mindset. No matter the knowledge you acquire or the plan you put together, without the right mindset, you'll likely end up back where you started, if you manage to get going at all.

The biggest change I made at age forty-seven wasn't quitting my job to buy properties; it was changing my mindset. I went on a rampage of reading books and going to seminars. I went to Peak Potentials seminars (created by T. Harv Eker, author of *Secrets of the Millionaire Mind*, one of my favorite books on the subject) like Guerilla Business School, World's Greatest Marketing Seminar, Enlightened Warrior Training, Wizard Training, Master Your Mind, and countless others. I also attended several Anthony Robbins seminars—such as Unleash the Power Within, Business Mastery, Life and Wealth Mastery, and more—to better understand myself and grow my box. What I realized is that your mindset can enable your success or keep you from it. It's that powerful!

I like to say, "The instructions on how to get out of your box *are* out of your box." Think about it for a moment. You need to break out of the limited box you reside in if you want to gain the knowledge you require to permanently escape from your box.

My hope is to help you young readers—even if you already have self-confidence—to better understand how your mind works, how you've been limited, and how to get outside your box. When you do that, it opens the door to the next stage of being able to grow your wealth. The more you understand your mind, your underlying blueprint, and your limitations, the faster your wealth can grow.

Along with the right mindset, you also need to understand how money works, which is what we'll cover in the second section of this book. I mentioned earlier that you're truly wealthy when you're making money while you sleep, but you'll never get there until you understand the basics of money and making it work for you.

You might be taking macro- or microeconomics classes, but based on the number of students I've interviewed coming out of school, I bet you're not being taught basic concepts, like return on investment or the magic of compound interest.

I want to help you lay the financial foundation that is

crucial to building wealth. You don't need to be a genius to become a millionaire, but you do need to understand money.

THE FORMULA FOR CREATING WEALTH

In the third section of the book, we'll look at how wealth is built. To do this, we're going to use a formula I came up with called C.R.E.A.T.E.™ Here's how it breaks down.

C: COMPOUNDING

To become wealthy, you must be able to multiply your money quickly. To do that, you need to understand compound interest. Once you do, you'll know why Einstein praised its power.

R: RETURN ON INVESTMENT

When you invest, you need to look for the highest possible return on that investment. Many people look only at cashflow, but most of your returns come in other areas. There's a magic formula we'll look at that will show you ROI is not what you think it is.

E: EXECUTION

This is huge. It is the key ingredient. Without this, nothing else you do will matter. Execution requires understanding your mind, getting beyond your barriers, dealing with fear, and not procrastinating. Executing is not *ready, aim, ready, aim, ready, aim,* and never firing. Action is crucial because you only get one life. You're going to make mistakes, but when you do, you'll adjust and continue forward. Success is not a straight line to the top. It's a curved line that goes up and down but ultimately takes you to the top.

A: ASSETS

You need to accumulate assets, which are things that bring money your way. The more assets you have and the larger they are, the faster you can build wealth.

T: TAXES

Taxes slow down the compounding effect substantially, which means you need to reduce the amount of taxes you're paying now. Usually that means deferring taxes to a later date, but it starts with understanding the tax code and taking advantage of it in a legal way. The government will get its money, just not right away. You'll use it first to build your wealth.

E: EMOTIONAL INTELLIGENCE

We know that a high IQ is not required to become wealthy. It's more important to have emotional intelligence, which means understanding your emotions and being able to bring empathy into your relationships. When you have strong relationships—with mentors, business partners, investors, lenders, and more—you're able to get stuff done. Additionally, when you have emotional intelligence, you are able to make better decisions based not on emotional states but on a rational, common sense state of mind.

WEALTH HELPS YOU PURSUE ANY PASSION

There are many ways to become wealthy, but in this book, we'll be looking at how real estate fulfills the C.R.E.A.T.E.™ Formula. Make no mistake, though—everything we'll look at, including this formula, can be used to pursue whatever life you want. I would never tell you to set aside your passion in pursuit of wealth. What I will tell you is to parallel your efforts, because wealth makes it easier to pursue your passion, whatever it might be.

It really is this simple: WEALTH = FREEDOM. Freedom allows you to do the things you want to do, help the people or causes you choose, and live the life you dream of.

For example, my son, Evan, wants to get into the film industry. My advice to him is to build his wealth while pursuing his passion for filmmaking. That way, he can finance his own movies one day. Wealth doesn't have to be his sole focus, but it should be part of what he's doing.

Wealth can enable the life of your dreams. It creates freedom for you to pursue your passion, which makes it as vital to life as your right arm or left leg. Despite what some people say, money is not evil. Wealthy people aren't all greedy or money hungry.

The more money you have, the more you're able to help people and benefit the world. Look at the work Bill Gates is doing to change the health of millions of people across the planet. I'm sure Gates would be doing that work even if he weren't a billionaire, but his vast wealth amplifies his impact. When used the right way, wealth can positively impact the world. It's allowed me to write this book and share my knowledge with the world. It's allowed me to support the building of a school. When I have new dreams in the future, it'll support those as well.

If being able to help people and having the freedom to pursue the life of your dreams gets you fired up, you're reading the right book. Let's dive into Chapter One and see the mindset you'll need to close your first deal, buy your first building, and make your first million.

GOLDEN EGGS

Later in the book, I'll talk about growing your golden goose, which produces your golden eggs. In simple terms, the golden eggs represent passive income leading to financial freedom. After each chapter in this book, you will find golden eggs (summary points) to help remind you of the highlights (or nuggets) in each section.

Here are the golden eggs for the introduction:

- Start building wealth when you're young. There's no minimum age to get started.
- The difference between making $50,000 a year and $1 million a year is awareness.
- Your mindset is the key ingredient to becoming wealthy. It is also the only thing holding you back.
- You must understand the incredible power of compound interest! It is the most powerful force in the universe according to Albert Einstein.
- There is no expiry date for success. I went from zero to multimillionaire starting at age forty-seven.
- Change your limiting mindset and acquire knowledge. Read quality books and attend seminars and courses.
- Learn the C.R.E.A.T.E.™ Formula.
- Wealth gives you FREEDOM to pursue your passion and to help people. The more money you have, the more people you can help.

- Break out of your limiting box. A beautiful, exciting world awaits you beyond its walls.
- Your money mindset was seeded when you were young. It is created by what you've heard your parents and teachers say and what you've witnessed and experienced. It's not set in stone and can be changed.
- You alone set the limits on where your life will lead you and how far you will go.
- A positive mindset is empowering. More importantly, it's a choice!

CHAPTER ONE

BREAK OUT OF THE BOX

Why in the hell did it take me forty-seven years to get off the corporate fast track and start pursuing my dreams of becoming a multimillionaire through real estate investing?

That's a question I ask myself often. During those years, I worked in real estate as an agent and made my clients millions of dollars through their investments. Why did I never see what was right in front of my face? I could've started buying properties in my twenties!

The reasons run deep, snaking all the way back to my childhood.

My father invested in real estate, and when I was a teenager, he used to cry poverty all the time. The buildings were *always* losing money. We grew up in a household of scarcity where my parents vacationed on the cheap and I knew better than to ask my dad for money.

I didn't know until I was older that my dad had been making good money with his real estate investments and chose to hide it from us. Even my mother believed that he was not a millionaire and the buildings weren't producing much. She became so indoctrinated with this belief that it persisted into her later years until the truth finally came out, which might explain why certain people in my family thought I was dealing drugs when I mentioned I'd made millions in real estate!

My father demonstrated a mindset of scarcity. Rather than teaching us money is abundant, he loudly and clearly articulated exactly the opposite. Scarcity oozed out of him, and like a contagious parasite, it infected my mother, my siblings, and me. It permeated my consciousness and created my money mindset, or how I think about money.

I always believed in my heart I would be a millionaire one day, but after forty-seven years of working hard and following the rules, I'd built zero wealth. Turns out there was nothing wrong with me. My money mindset had been holding me back the entire time.

Despite working with wealthy investors, I didn't pursue

real estate in my twenties, because every time I thought about buying a building, I heard my dad's voice in my head saying, "The buildings aren't making any money. In fact, they are losing money, so our family doesn't have much."

Without realizing it, my father taught me that owning real estate was a losing endeavor filled with difficulties and negative cashflow. I believed him for forty-seven long, frustrating years.

The day I called "bullcrap" on my money mindset was the day my life changed.

HOW OUR MONEY MINDSET DEVELOPS

We all have a money mindset, that ruling belief system that dictates how we think about money. For most of us, we're programmed with these beliefs at a young age.

Growing up, do you remember your parents saying anything like the following?

"We can't afford that..."

"Money doesn't grow on trees..."

"Rich people are crooks..."

"Money is hard to come by..."

If so, these attitudes contribute to a mindset that can carry over into adulthood if you're not careful. You don't think about this when you're young, but your mindset, and where you decide to direct your awareness, means everything. What you focus on expands.

This is how the mind works. What we think about most dictates our reality. The way we think and act, our behaviors, positive or negative attitudes, fear—they all bubble up from the programming we receive at a young age and the belief system that develops as a result.

The adults who influence our mindset, like our parents and teachers, are not trying to hurt us by passing along these beliefs. This is done unconsciously. I truly believe my parents and teachers wanted the best for me and did everything they could to help me succeed in life. For the most part, they were simply passing along the programming they'd received when they were kids.

Teachers are, for the most part, just following the curriculum set out for them by the school board or university. Unfortunately, school in general has not adjusted to the rapidly changing times, at least not fast enough. It's like shifting the course of a giant ship. It takes much energy and time.

I have three kids, and I often think about the beliefs I passed along to them when they were young. I've shared new beliefs with them since throwing off my old mindset, some really empowering ones, but my old beliefs may still be lingering to some extent.

As kids, we don't just listen to what our parents say. We also watch what they do, which means our negative programming can originate from observing the way our parents make money. If they work long hours for little pay, we can begin to believe them when they say money is hard to come by, because their actions back up their words.

If you're a young person, as you leave college and enter the workforce, pay attention to how many of your friends live in the same sort of neighborhood as their parents, have the same kinds of jobs, and make the same amount of money. What you'll see is the damaging effect of a money mindset with a ceiling. If your friends grow up thinking $50,000 of yearly income is the best they can do, more than likely they'll never make more than $50,000 a year.

YOU MUST STOP LIMITING YOURSELF

The biggest problem with a money mindset ruled by beliefs like "money is scarce" or "money is hard to make" is how limiting it can be. When we believe these lies, we box ourselves into a reality that's utterly false and yet consumes our lives.

I'm reminded of the book *The Untethered Soul* by Michael Singer. It's a beautiful book that I highly recommend everyone read. In it, Singer talks about life in a unique way. He says you're born into this beautiful pasture with trees, warm air, sunny skies, and flowers everywhere. You decide to build a house, and in the beginning, you leave the windows wide open to the world outside. Eventually, you decide to close the windows to protect the house and your belongings inside. Over time, you close the blinds and turn on the lights.

Finally, the lights are turned off, and the inside is only lit by a candle. Your reality becomes a dark box. It's all you see, so it becomes all you know. You lose awareness of the flowers, the pasture, the sky, and the beautiful world outside that you left to be inside the house.

Singer uses this analogy to describe how people close themselves off to the world until they're in a tiny box that's become their new reality. That's life for most people.

Getting out of that box is hard because most people don't even know they're in a box or don't have awareness of what's outside it. They have no idea how limited they are.

A negative money mindset can box us in and keep us from becoming wealthy if we believe the false programming we received in our younger years. Is it true that money is scarce? Trillions of dollars are out there, and multimillionaires are made every day. Is money hard to get? A lot of new millionaires aren't any smarter than you, and many didn't go to school. What they do have, however, is awareness and supportive belief systems.

If you're reading this book, you're good enough to become a millionaire or a billionaire if you want. Don't believe the lie that you're a bad person if you want to become wealthy or that you're not good enough to become wealthy.

Money isn't evil; money is good. In fact, I'd argue that money is a spiritual thing. It gives you the power to do more for yourself and for others. It gives you the freedom to create the reality you want in this very wonderful opportunity we've been given called life.

In a previous book, I wrote about two important things. One is that you're blessed with something very special, which is simply your life. The odds of even being alive and on this earth are infinitesimal. It's a miracle that you are alive when billions didn't make it. Two, your life span is very short, much shorter than you think.

So, because life is special and very brief, you really need

to get it right! If you're a young person, now is the time to ask yourself what you want from life, how you're going to achieve it, and what beliefs might be holding you back. Don't make the same mistake I did and let a false mindset drive your decisions for forty-seven years.

When I meet a young person who's looking to build their wealth, I like to offer them a deal. When they ask what it is, I reply, "I'll give you my entire net worth right now. You'll get every building, my house, my bank account, and all the investments I have. All I ask for in return is one thing."

At this point, they're filled with wide-eyed excitement. They ask me, "What is it?"

I tell them, "I want your age."

As I've said, time is the ultimate X factor. If you've got the time, all that's necessary to build wealth is the information and the proper mindset. Anybody can get there, but it starts with understanding who you are, what rules you, and what you need to change.

A POSITIVE MONEY MINDSET IS EMPOWERING

If a negative money mindset holds us back, then the opposite must be true: a positive money mindset can move us forward. If I created a line graph charting my wealth-building journey, you'd see that the line started moving upward when I tore down my old mindset and rebuilt a new one with beliefs that supported my pursuit of wealth.

I could have started this book with financial basics or real estate investment strategies, but I'm covering mindset first because you can't build lasting wealth if negative beliefs are weighing you down. Sure, you might be able to tread water for a while, but if you don't shake loose of those anchors, you'll eventually be dragged down by them.

Why do you think it is that wealthy people remain wealthy even when their circumstances change? It's not because they've discovered the secret formula for getting rich.

Wealthy people remain wealthy because they have a positive money mindset.

If you were to take away every dime Richard Branson has, what do you think would happen? I think he would recoup his fortune very quickly, because he's programmed to do so.

T. Harv Eker uses the term "thermostat" to describe how much money people are capable of handling or think they deserve to make. Earlier, I mentioned that some kids you know will end up making $50,000 a year because that's how much money their parents make. Their thermostat is set at that level because it's where they feel comfortable.

I'll bet you've heard the stories of people who win tens of millions of dollars through the lottery, only to return to their previous level of wealth within a few years. How the hell does that happen? It happens because their thermostat is set to tens of thousands, not tens of millions. Even after a spike that significant, their financial temperature eventually levels back out, because that's where the lottery winner feels comfortable.

Billionaires like Buffett, Musk, and Branson have thermostats set at billions. They're not stopping at millions, because they know they're capable of making decisions, forming relationships, and getting into the types of businesses that can make them a billion dollars very quickly.

We need to model ourselves after successful wealth builders, because they leave clues. You can either spend your whole life making mistakes as you try to become wealthy, or you can follow the trails of crumbs wealthy people left behind while building massive fortunes.

Learning from them will shorten the time it takes to get where you want to be.

Multimillionaires and billionaires seek to learn new things every day. They don't stop just because they're rich. Buffett spends five hours reading per day, which offers us a clue about the importance of learning, even for someone at the apex of extreme wealth.

If successful people are learning all the time, shouldn't you be learning, too?

HOW TO CHANGE YOUR MONEY MINDSET

We've peeled back the onion on the source of a scarcity mindset. We know how it develops, why it's faulty, and that a positive money mindset can help move you forward.

Following that is the question: can we change our money mindset?

The answer is a resounding yes! Let me show you how.

The first thing that you need to do is become aware of your money mindset. Look inward, and recognize the beliefs you hold about money that might be holding you back.

As you spot these beliefs, write them down on a sheet of paper.

If you know your mindset is faulty, accept that the limiting box you live in will remain dark and closed off until you throw the doors and windows open and let information in.

Acknowledging your negative money mindset is the first step to changing it.

After you finish with your limiting beliefs about money, it's time to examine the negative thoughts you have about yourself. Maybe you think you're not good enough or you don't deserve to be loved. Maybe you're scared to be successful or fear that success is out of reach for you. Maybe you feel like your children or grandchildren might get there but not you.

When you finish writing down these limiting beliefs— both financial and personal—ask yourself this question: are they true? I did this myself. Growing up, I was a Canadian record holder in swimming and on the honor roll in school, and I stayed out of trouble.

Yet due to a lack of validation from my parents, especially my father, I had the pervasive feeling that I wasn't good enough. Nothing I did seemed to be acceptable to my father. He always found fault in what I did, and nothing I did could help me shake that feeling of failure.

Later in life, I finally asked myself the question: is it true that I'm not good enough?

The answer was so obvious for me, and it will be for you, too.

The false beliefs I held were not only untrue—they were downright absurd!

These underlying beliefs suddenly seemed so ridiculous that I laughed at them, yet for the first five decades of my life, they were no laughing matter. It was a liberating moment to let go of the faulty beliefs that had long held me captive by ruling my thoughts and actions and limiting my success.

Once I did, I realized that I am every bit as capable as the millionaires and billionaires who were already out there. I have the skills and the personality, and now, I have the mindset. I have what it takes to be wealthy, and I'm more than good enough to achieve my goals.

You need to do this, too. Look directly in the mirror at yourself and say it out loud: "I am more than good enough. I am successful." Repeat this as if you have already achieved your success. Feel it!

Repeat that every morning at least ten times, and as time passes, you will rebuild your belief system. Those words will become your new reality as they sink into your subconscious mind. You can create similar affirmations for every one of the belief systems that hold you back.

We also need to replace your faulty beliefs about money with new, positive beliefs. Maybe you were raised to believe money is the root of all evil, so wealthy people must be evil.

When you look at this belief for long enough, it starts to fall apart. Yes, there are rich people out there who are lowlifes, but that's true of people who are poor, too.

Think about Bill Gates, one of the richest people in the world. If money truly is evil, he should be one of the vilest human beings on the planet. Yet through his foundation, Gates donates billions every year to health and education initiatives all over the globe. The same holds true for Elon Musk. He's a billionaire, yet he has done so much for the environment with his push toward new battery technologies for vehicles. In fact, he has allowed his competition access to his technology in an effort to help mankind and the planet.

Money itself is a tool, so it's not inherently good or evil. Oftentimes, an abundance of money amplifies someone's character, so for someone like Gates, his generous spirit can be amplified to levels that most people can only dream of reaching.

Is it true that money is hard to get? Only if you lack awareness. Once you become aware of the paths that lead to wealth, you can begin down the one that suits you best. I'm guessing part of the reason you picked up this book is to learn how to build wealth through real estate. Once you know what to do, the only thing holding you back will be inaction.

Let's look at some other ways we can continue to transform our money mindset.

FEED YOUR BRAIN NEW INFORMATION

In addition to replacing faulty beliefs, you must start feeding your brain new information.

Here's why: your bank account will never exceed the balance of your brain account. It is as simple as that! If you wonder why your bank account isn't as big as you had hoped, it is because your brain account is limited and requires more deposits.

Building wealth must begin with your brain account. Making consistent deposits of tested information, mentoring, awareness, and practice will grow your brain account, which, in turn, will proportionately grow your bank account. Think deeply about this!

I like to make deposits into my brain account through books and seminars.

When I was going through my personal transformation at age forty-seven, I read a lot of books. When I say a lot, I mean well over a hundred books on various topics: psychology, success, motivation, money, real estate, health. At the end of this book, I've included a list of some of my favorite books that will help you understand how your mind works and how to build wealth.

If you want to change your money mindset, you must start attending seminars and courses. Doing so fed my brain new information and experiences that I couldn't have gotten elsewhere.

I remember buying a seminar package from T. Harv Eker's Peak Potentials. Like many people, I was skeptical at first, but those experiences were transformative. If you looked at the line graph charting my financial success, you'd see a big spike after I began attending those seminars.

When you start talking about seminars, a lot of the same critiques come up, the most popular being that they aren't effective at creating lasting change. This is a familiar refrain I hear from people when I invite them to come with me to see T. Harv Eker, Tony Robbins, or other great mentors: "Seminars are exciting and energizing. I love every moment of it. Then I return home, and the feeling lasts for a few days—and then I go back to normal, and nothing happens."

These people are all missing a critical piece: execution. You can have all the ingredients for an amazing meal, but if you never start cooking, you're going to go hungry.

The people who approach seminars with genuine passion and determination, the ones who say, "I will do whatever it takes to change my life, and I'm not going back to my old life," can create a brighter reality for themselves when they get home and put into action what they learn.

I can say that with certainty because I was one of those people! When I turned down the new executive role with the Montreal company I mentioned, I was declaring to myself and the world: *I'm all in. There's no going back. I'll do whatever it takes to find a better way forward.*

Making deposits into my brain account through books and seminars is part of that better way forward. If you are prepared to do the work required by what you read in books and what you learn at seminars, I'm confident that the new awareness will change your life.

OBSERVE YOUR THOUGHTS

As you shed your old beliefs and feed your brain new information, pay attention to the thoughts you have. The old "you" won't go down without a fight, so you'll likely find a running commentary in your mind as you go about making changes in your life.

Practice self-observation to see what kind of thoughts you're having. What you might find is that the voice in your head—which is your ego, NOT you—is full of crap.

In *The Untethered Soul*, Michael Singer says if you were sitting on a park bench and the voice in your head was spoken from the mouth of someone sitting beside you, your likely reaction would be to get up and run away as fast as you could, because you'd think that person was insane.

Begin to pay attention to the voice in your head, because it's not always speaking to your best interests. Our ego doesn't want us to grow emotionally, spiritually, or financially. It wants to maintain the status quo, and it will trick you into remaining there. Your ego knows you better than anybody. It knows your innermost thoughts and works to keep you from changing. It will manipulate you to maintain the status quo so it can live on. It will say and do whatever is required to keep you tethered to your comfort zone. Watch this very closely in yourself and other people around you. Growth is uncomfortable and difficult! This is how people become acclimated to their own misery. It amazes me how many people would rather be comfortable in their misery than be uncomfortable with growth and success.

Pay attention to what's going on in your head. What you'll find—and what we'll work on in Chapter Three—is that you can control it instead of letting it stream endlessly.

Self-hypnosis is helpful in dealing with unwanted thoughts. Don't worry; I'm not going to ask you to dangle a pocket watch in front of your face or dance around like a chicken.

Self-hypnosis is nothing more than repeating certain things to yourself. John Kehoe, a great mentor of mine, wrote *Mind Power into the 21st Century*, in which he outlines six laws that rule the mind. We covered one of those laws earlier: you can purge any thought from your mind and insert another thought of your choice. If you have negative or limiting thoughts, you can replace them with positive thoughts that will serve you and help you grow. Understand that your mind cannot tell the difference between what is real and what is imaginary. This is quite profound.

We can all do this, though most of us don't because it takes some effort.

Instead, we allow the same thoughts to bubble up day after day from our negative belief systems. Would you believe that more than 85 percent of our thoughts are almost identical to those from the previous day? How can you possibly grow, change, and succeed in life if the same negative, non-serving thoughts constantly dominate your mind? Don't listen passively to the voices trying to keep you where things are comfortable. Get UNcomfortable!

You were born with no limitations and a positive perspective on life. Negativity in your thinking, which affects your actions, is a result of bad software being installed on the hard drive that is your brain. In this chapter, we've seen how you can remove that corrupt software and install new software that gets your mind running as it was intended.

In the next chapter, we'll look at how that super computer in your head—your mind—is the greatest tool you have for manifesting the change you want to make in your life.

GOLDEN EGGS

- Anyone can be a millionaire. You just need an average IQ and awareness.
- Your money mindset has a thermostat that keeps you where you are.
- Your mindset is based on your belief systems. Do they serve you? If not, change them!
- Successful people leave clues. Learn from them, and save years of mistakes and pain.
- Observe your thoughts. The "limiting you" will not

go away easily. Purge negative or limiting thoughts, and replace them with empowering ones.

- Take action on what you learn. An idea without action is only an idea.

CHAPTER TWO

MANIFEST YOUR REALITY

I want to be crystal clear: it takes time and effort to change your reality. However, the moment you decide to change your reality, you have already begun the change!

Kehoe described the process of changing your reality in a way that always resonated with me. John asked readers to picture a three-foot-high vat of clear water. Now, imagine dropping a single drop of red dye into that vat.

What happens? The answer is nothing. The water remains clear.

Instead of stopping after that first drop, you add a single drop of red dye into the vat of water each day. You don't notice any change for many days, but then you perceive the water changing from clear to the lightest tone of pink.

Over time, as you continue to put red drops in the water, the entire vat of water slowly goes from pink to red.

Manifesting your new reality works much the same way. You can't snap your fingers and be exactly where you want to be in life, especially if, like me, you've spent many years forming bad habits and making subpar choices. It will take time for things to change. If you persist, it will absolutely work, but the result won't manifest in front of your face right away.

Your life is ultimately but a reflection of your thoughts. It's that simple! Success really comes down to one straightforward concept: your predominant thoughts create your reality. Understand this and you're more than halfway to where you want to be. The rest is just execution.

There was never anything that did not proceed from a thought.

RALPH WALDO EMERSON

For decades, I banged my head against the wall, doing the same thing repeatedly while expecting a different result. (*Hello, Bob, meet insanity.*) I was like many successful people: smart, capable, skilled, and overdelivering—but I had nothing to show for it.

Finally, I stopped repeating mistakes. Like you, I decided to change. I began a journey to understand what was necessary in order to effect change. With that decision alone, my life began to shift. I got off the road I'd been traveling at the next exit.

I started adding drops of red dye to the vat that is my mind. I went to seminars, read books, and changed my thinking. It would be easy to say the external changes that happened in my life began when I partnered with Norm and started buying property, but the truth is, the internal changes I made long before buying my first building created my new reality.

Your mind really is the greatest tool at your disposal for creating lasting change. In fact, if you try to create external changes in your life—big house, nice cars, fancy clothes—before you make internal changes, you're destined to end up back where you are now.

How can I say that with confidence? I've watched it happen in my own life.

I have a friend (let's call him Mike) who is constantly looking to change his financial situation, which is dire. Mike has never been married, and he won't date women, because he feels that he needs money to go out on dates. But every time I tell him, "You've got to invest in your inner world, your mind," he doesn't hear me. Mike makes the mistake of "investing" in his outer world instead. He believes that if he buys the right stock or finds the right business opportunity, he'll make the money needed to change his reality.

I implored Mike to work on his inner world by attending seminars with me, but he refused. He never reads the books I suggest. Despite counseling him for many years, he's in the same position today (or worse) as when I first met him. I know Mike is frustrated by his lack of progress, but the truth is he keeps hammering the wrong end of the nail.

At this point, I'd like to remind you about the power of your thoughts and their intrinsic vibrations. Basically, the thoughts you think will attract similar thoughts and vibrations. In other words, if you are on a roll of thinking negative thoughts, you will attract more negative thoughts and more negative circumstances. If you are thinking positive, productive thoughts, you will attract more positive thoughts and manifest positive circumstances into your reality. Ever hear the saying "Success leads to success"? Similarly, if you think negative thoughts, you will have a profoundly negative effect on everyone and everything around you.

YOUR MIND IS A POWERFUL INSTRUMENT

One of the reasons people like Mike don't use their minds

to create change is that they fail to realize their mind is an instrument. They believe they *are* their minds and that their thoughts control their actions. In fact, the opposite is true.

Your mind is an instrument you can control. Remember what we discussed last chapter: the voice in your head is mostly full of crap. Your mind spews random, unedited, nonsense comments like a twenty-four-hour TV channel. Like any good TV channel, your mind wants to keep you glued to the thoughts it produces. Don't forget that you can turn it off, just like a TV. Better yet, you can change the channel to something that enriches your life.

To create a new reality for yourself, your thoughts should be supportive of the reality you're trying to create. Anything that bubbles up and threatens the change you're trying to create should be tossed aside. It comes from a place of fear, not faith.

Your mind is a tool to wield as you see fit. The process of changing your thoughts might be time-consuming and difficult, but I promise it's worth the effort. When I quit my job and suddenly had to provide for my family with no steady paycheck, what kind of thoughts do you think ran through my head on a daily basis? It was fearful thinking 24/7.

I had to stop allowing thoughts that made me feel weak,

unhappy, and trapped. I told myself daily that I was in charge, not my mind. I was not a slave to my thoughts. I could change them to provide me with strength, courage, and encouragement.

Once you get a handle on your thoughts, you can begin feeding the instrument atop your shoulders new information that will aid you in changing your external reality.

That's where the resources we talked about in the last chapter come into play: books, seminars, and affirmations. If you're a young person who grew up on the internet, you might know of blogs, YouTube channels, or social media influencers who can aid you in this process of transformation. We're going to talk in the second and third sections of this book about the specifics of real estate investing, but if you've not cultivated a fertile mind that is ready for the seeds of new information, you won't reap the kind of harvest you want.

FEEDING YOUR MIND

One of the key actions you must take in order to expand your world is to constantly nourish your mind with diverse, high-quality information. Your mind loves variety and wants all its senses to experience the thrill of learning. As I have been professing, begin by reading. It's essential on your journey of growth to read empowering books. Everything you read enters your subconscious mind by osmosis and adds to the already large database of information you can draw from. The more you read and expand your database, the larger your box, the grander your dreams, the better your decisions, and the more deliberate your actions will become.

Choose to read books that give you a wide-ranging perspective. Pick books that enlighten and motivate you. Read books on personal development, books that inspire you, and books on business and money. Choose books that are central to your passion and life focus. The bottom line is, read, read, read—whenever you get the chance. Another way is to listen to books. I love this approach as I can listen to books in my car, in bed before I go to sleep, when I wake up, or even in the shower.

Think of your mind as a supercomputer. The more data you feed it, the more efficient it will become. And if you stick to high-quality data, the answers generated by this amazing machine called your brain will also be of higher quality. Choose good books, and read as many as you can.

SEMINARS, YOUR SUBCONSCIOUS, AND YOU

For those of you who think seminars are a waste of time and money, or who wonder whether the seminars you've been attending truly have an effect on your life, do not wonder anymore. The fact is, seminars can have a significant effect on your life. In some cases, seminars provide you with the information, guidance, and insights you need to immediately effect the change you are seeking. In other cases, they open your mind to new ideas and new ways of thinking, just like my book might do for you. But in all cases, the information you receive at these seminars enters your subconscious mind, expanding the database on which you subconsciously rely. Like a computer, the more information you program into the subconscious, the better the quality of the output and the quicker it can offer you the guidance and answers you seek.

If you are serious about changing your life for the better, it is vital that you come to a clear understanding of how the subconscious mind works and how it creates your reality. We've already seen some of the ways in which this happens, but I now want to caution you. Though you can change your perception of reality almost instantaneously, and though conscious action can lead to some quick changes, it takes time and practice to change your subconscious mind. There is no magic pill; it's about changing belief systems and habits and creating new ones. If you think you can permanently change your mind and your reality in a matter of moments and without effort, you are mistaken. Changing your reality takes work and time, but it's definitely worth it.

The good news is that if you are diligent and persistent

in your commitment, you can absolutely change and create the life of your dreams. Once you imprint new information or habits into your subconscious mind, using the information and insights you gain from attending high-quality seminars, the information becomes a permanent part of the ongoing process of change and growth. What's more, seminars are alive and active. They recruit all your senses and emotions, allowing you to retain much more information. They stimulate a frame of mind that's uplifting and energizing, and they place you in a frame of mind in which epiphanies can occur, blasting out the sides of your present box. Remember, some of the greatest masters began by attending seminars, and most continue their growth by continually attending them. For those of you who are already on the right path toward your goals or already have excellent parental role models, I urge you to reread the above. It pertains to you as well. This process of feeding your subconscious supercomputer will catapult you to higher heights and at a faster pace.

THIS LIFE BELONGS TO YOU, NOT ANYONE ELSE

Having three children of my own, I spend a lot of time speaking with young adults. When I ask them about their plans for life and what they want to do, I hear quite often that young people feel like they're being pushed down a particular path by their parents or teachers, which creates a feeling of disempowerment. Instead of feeling free, they feel cornered.

If you feel this way, don't miss what I'm about to say: your life is not predetermined.

The choices made by others don't have to define the direction of your life. We're raised by our parents and in school to do what we're told, but when it comes to charting your course, you don't have to do everything you're told all the time. Take control of the blank canvas you were given at birth. Don't forget that life is very short and you're blessed to be here.

The gift of life is yours, and you're now on a journey to create the life you want.

This is not the life of your parents, teachers, or friends. It's your life. Your parents and teachers can help by acting as guides, but in the end, it's your journey.

If you're a young person, I don't want you to feel that your parents or teachers are bad people. On the contrary, they only want you to be happy and successful. Often, adults in our lives want to keep us from experiencing pain, especially the pain they experienced, so they'll push us toward safe career paths that provide a steady paycheck. Unless they're entrepreneurially minded, the idea of making money through real estate probably scares them to death.

Don't dismiss the wisdom that adults pass on to you in your life. They've made their own mistakes and have learned through personal pain. Their stories and experiences can provide you with important lessons if you open your mind and listen. Take what they share and test it against what you want for your life. Just remember that if you're determined to chart your own course, you're not predestined to follow in anyone's footsteps.

The universe places no limits on you. You can succeed in any way you believe you can. You may come from a low-income background where you were programmed to think, "Well, this is just the way my life is going to be." Don't believe that false programming.

By harnessing the power of your mind, you can throw off the yoke of imposed limits and create a beautiful life for you and for your family. I know, because I did it.

That brings me to an important point: older adults aren't boxed into their current reality, either. Whatever limits you feel are holding you back can be broken: a dead-end career, poisonous relationships, poor mental or physical health, a lack of expertise, and more.

It begins with casting aside false beliefs about yourself, changing the thoughts that fill your head, and feeding the instrument that is your mind with new information. Once you've laid that foundation, the next question to answer is: *what exactly do I want?*

DETERMINE YOUR DESIRES

You're reading this book because you want to make a positive change in your life. If you're a young person, you want to break free of any preconceived notions society has for you regarding the ways you'll make money in your lifetime. If you're an older adult stuck in a job where you're working hard and building zero wealth (like I was), you're ready to take the next exit and find a new road to travel.

Wanting to build wealth through real estate is fantastic, but before you start buying buildings, you must first ask yourself why you want to be wealthy. Why do you want to make this change that is going to produce massive, life-altering results?

A lot of people jump straight to the "how" without fully fleshing out their "why."

They know they want to build wealth, maybe through real estate, but their first thought is *how in the world am I going to do this?* Instead, their first thought should be *why do I want to do this?* Here's the reason the "why" must come first: if your "why" is big enough, then the "how" naturally follows. Your "why" gives you incredible power and momentum.

Your desire is key. Change doesn't simply happen because you have a thought. Change happens because you are uncomfortable, discontented, unhappy, and disconnected on a daily basis. You yearn deeply for change. Desire is important; it underpins your motivation and drive, which will propel you forward and toward a better life.

What are your desires? What are you looking for in your life?

Here, you need to divorce yourself from what others want you to be or do. Take time to genuinely connect with yourself and consider these questions: Who am I? What is my mission on earth? What are my gifts? What are my skills? What do I love?

This is a critically important exercise for young people. The teenagers I've talked with often fall into one of two categories: they were streamed in a particular direction early on in their life (perhaps following in their parents' footsteps), or they're generalists who become acquainted with many different interests, but because they never drilled down into something that sparked their interest, they exit high school lacking direction.

If you're a young person, I encourage you to take some time to think about who you are, to look at your skillset, and to consider what direction you want your life to take. You'll know when you're on the right track, because deep inside, your heart will feel good.

It's true that the bigger your desire is for something, the better chance you have to manifest that reality. You need to fervently, passionately hunger for your goal. In order to create the reality you want, you also need to create the energy to want it powerfully.

GET SPECIFIC WITH YOUR GOALS

I was once at a seminar where participants were given an exercise. We were asked to make a "why" list, meaning the things that moved and motivated us. I went nuts and listed everything from "empowering my kids" and "traveling the world" to "building a school." I had two full pages of "whys" that excited me to the core.

Later, when I spoke with a gentleman from that group, he said the exercise frustrated him. When I asked why, he answered, "Because I couldn't list a single why!"

My heart grieved for this guy. As I considered why he struggled with the exercise, my gut told me he couldn't list anything because the life he was envisioning was hazy and undefined. As a result, it didn't fire him up. On the other hand, when I thought about the future I wanted for myself and my family, I saw it with 20/20 vision. I had a burning desire in my soul to manifest that reality, which translated into two pages of "whys."

Desires go hand-in-hand with specific goals. Vague notions won't get you very far. You need to be crystal clear on what you want for your life, because it is those aspirations that will fuel you when a deal falls through or you suffer a financial setback.

Drill down into the details here. What net worth do you want? One million? One hundred million? Don't be timid. It's possible to achieve any reality you want.

What kind of house do you want to live in? What car do you want to drive?

Do you want to travel the world? If so, where do you want to go first?

With these specific goals in mind, take a step back and ask yourself why you want these things. For wealthy people, money is often a tool to achieve something greater.

There's nothing wrong with wanting to be rich and letting that fuel you, of course. But what you'll often see is that the wealthiest people are driven by goals bigger than themselves:

I grew up in a poor household, and I don't want my family to go through that.

I want to buy a gorgeous new home for my parents, who helped me get to this point.

I want to make a billion dollars so I can help doctors and scientists cure cancer.

Goals and desires go hand in hand. When you lack one or the other, you'll end up like the guy I met at the seminar who left a "why" exercise with a blank page.

HARNESS THE POWER OF A VISION BOARD

One way to help you stay focused on your goals and desires is to create a vision board. Like seminars, vision boards get a bad rap for being corny. What I would say to the people who question the power of a vision board is that they're afraid to own what they want. They're scared of putting their heart's desires on a board for the world to see.

When you get down to it, that's what a vision board is

all about. There's no mystical power attached to pinning images on a corkboard or piece of plywood. What you're tapping into when you create this board is the power of visualization and positive reinforcement. You're going to set this board somewhere so that you see it every day, preferably multiple times per day.

Each time you see it, you should experience the feeling of already having the things on that board present in your life. You're already living in that beautiful house, driving that fancy sports car, building that school, attaining your financial goal, or traveling to that exotic destination.

Vision boards are great because they can go anywhere: in your car, in your bedroom or office, or even online so you can see it on your computer or phone whenever you want.

Whether it's physical or virtual, pin the visual representations of what you wish to manifest in your life. The subjects or objects can be material, spiritual, or human.

You can pin the family you want to have, the romantic partner you hope to meet, the health you want, the workplace you want to go to every day. Anything that resonates with you should go on the board. Clip photos, graphics, or artwork and attach them to your board.

The important part of the vision board exercise is that

you need to practice feeling like these are present-tense achievements. Feel the images in the here and now.

If you have an image of your dream car, envision touching the car and driving it. Is it a smooth drive? Is it powerful? Drive it down streets or highways that you know. If you have an image of a house, imagine living in it. Walk through it. Sleep in the bedrooms. Play Snooker in the pool room. Eat in the kitchen. Have fun with the experience.

MY VISION BOARD EXPERIENCE

I'll tell you what happens over time from my own personal experience. I created a vision board using a blue Bristol board. I attached images from magazines: a house, a pool, a car, all sorts of things. My net worth was written down along with where I wanted to live.

The board was hung on the wall in front of my desk. At the beginning, I looked at it a lot. Eventually, I stopped paying close attention to it, although it was always there.

About two years later, I was working at my desk when my son came into my office, looked at my board, and said, "Gee, Dad, this thing has been up for a long time. I've never really looked at it. What is it? Why do you have a picture of your car there?"

I bolted up and went to the board. My son was right: there was a white Acura on my board just like the one I owned. I had always wanted a black car and never considered an Acura. Regardless, I now owned the car I'd pinned to my board two years earlier.

As I started looking at the other pictures I'd disregarded for so long, my hair stood up on end and I got goosebumps. It was as if my vision board had a mind of its own.

We had recently bought a house and completely renovated the back of it. We enlarged the wall in the back, installed massive sliding doors, and also put in a pool that was a unique shape. I couldn't believe it: on the board was a house with large sliding doors and a pool that was exactly like mine.

I was stunned. I went from picture to picture, and every single thing on that board had manifested itself into my reality. The only thing different on the board was my net worth.

I had pinned "$2 Million" to the board, and I had surpassed that number by quite a bit.

If you think a vision board sounds esoteric and weird, I'm here to tell you there is nothing weird about it. Some of the smartest, wealthiest people in the world create vision boards, including John Assaraf, whose vision board experience made national headlines.

John made a vision board with a photo from a magazine of a house in another state that he really liked. Years later, after moving all across the country, John found his old vision board. There, smack in the middle of the board, was a picture of the house he'd just moved into. Not a house like it—the exact house he'd pinned to his board all those years ago.

BEING IN THE RIGHT STATE OF MIND

Your state of mind is another critical piece of manifesting your reality.

We all have those days where we feel down in the dumps or wake up in a negative state of mind. I think humankind naturally leans toward negativity. It's a primal tendency that seems to be part of our process of dealing with challenges and overcoming them.

If you're trying to manifest a better reality, the state that you are in matters. Tony Robbins spends a lot of time talking about state of being, and rightly so. You are not glued to a negative mood. You can change your state in the snap of a finger.

An easy way to shift your mood is through movement. You're probably sitting in front of your computer for hours. You may not feel that great. Get up and do twenty jumping jacks. Go for a jog around your backyard or neighborhood. Get the blood flowing. You'll find your mood improves as endorphins are released by your brain during exercise.

Do you know what Tony Robbins does before he goes on stage? He jumps on a trampoline that's right off stage to get himself in a positive, high-energy state of mind.

Avoid making important decisions when you are in a negative state of mind. You will often make a mistake. The best decisions are made from a positive, high-energy state.

If you are in a position where a decision is required, try to alter your own state of mind before making that decision. Better decisions emerge from positive mindsets.

It doesn't matter what the decision is about—which university to choose, what car to buy, whatever it is. Transform your mindset from negative to positive. Try jumping, dancing, screaming, singing, or moving in some way, and then make your decision.

HAPPINESS IS A HABIT

It took me a long time to figure out that happiness is a

state of mind you choose on a daily basis, not a fleeting feeling you experience.

I used to be an unhappy person. People who saw me in my early adulthood thought I was a happy and positive guy. It was an exterior shell. I was suffering on the inside. Sometimes, you just live with underlying malaise and are unhappy for many different reasons.

I began to "exteriorize" happiness. I thought, if I'm rich, I'll be happy. If I marry the right girl, I'll be happy. If I have children, I'll be happy. Some random, future event dictated my state of mind. It took me a long time to realize that no outer event constructs your joy. In a negative state, you'll always be searching for the next thing to make you happy.

Books and blog posts on happiness are published every day, but a single message remains: happiness is a choice. It is a habit you must instill in yourself. You need to choose to be happy and work on it daily.

One way to get there is through the practice of gratitude. Identify the good things in your life, and put your awareness on them. Feel grateful for the things that are going well. Don't dismiss or ignore them. I keep a list by my bed of ten things that receive my gratitude.

Every few days, I switch up the list by adding or subtracting things for which I'm grateful. Start a list for yourself. Read that list as soon as you wake up in the morning. The aim is to remember all the things that make life worth living.

When you stop and genuinely feel gratitude, you internalize happiness on the spot. The cells of your body experience that joy. Continue doing it until it is a habit.

I've always felt that the good things given to us in life are gifts. If you don't acknowledge those gifts, you won't receive more. You must pay attention to them. When you're grateful for things you have by showing gratitude, more gifts will flow your way.

In almost every situation in life, we can find a way to frame an experience as either negative or positive. It's very important and life-affirming to always look for a positive spin on an event, no matter how difficult it appears to us at first. And remember: that positive spin will attract more positive thoughts and circumstances into your reality.

Maybe you're experiencing a lack of money today. One perspective is that you were meant to have this problem so that you would be challenged to undergo change and to manifest a new reality. When you finally achieve success, you'll be joyous.

I know that some people will say, "But that's hard to do. I'm dealing with really difficult issues. How could I choose to frame it in a positive way?"

My answer is that you need to think carefully. A difficult but revealing exercise is to inspect an issue and find the lesson in it. In every single situation I've faced, I've been able to identify a reason why it's happening and how it's actually positive.

Looking at the world this way can be difficult at first. But once you adopt this practice, it can bring you a level of happiness that you probably didn't have before in your life.

NOTHING HAPPENS WITHOUT ACTION

In the first chapter, we worked to shake off limiting mindsets, including those we have about money, and replace them with mindsets that empower us. In this chapter, we saw that manifesting a new reality requires knowing our desires, having specific goals, being in the right state of mind, and finding the good in every negative situation.

Now, it's time for the rubber to meet the road. We needed to start with mindset because that's the foundation of change, but nothing happens without action. You can have a great blueprint and a rock-solid foundation, but if you don't start building the house, you'll never have a place to live. Changing your life means getting your hands dirty.

Be aware before we start that this path to wealth is not paved; it's bumpy.

Many people start this process and tell me, "I get how the mind works. I have my vision board up. I'm jumping up and down in the morning to get into a positive state. I'm reading books and going to seminars." So far, so good. But then they say, "How come change isn't happening?" or "I'm experiencing some change, but it's too slow!"

The path to success isn't a straight line but a crooked, circuitous road that takes you on a journey. You're not buying an executive class seat; you're going on foot!

You will make mistakes along this journey. Understand those mistakes are an integral part of the journey. The secret to success is in the action and execution. You won't reach your destination effortlessly or painlessly. No journey that's worthwhile is like that.

In the next chapter, we'll see how to take action, move forward, and manage your fears as they come at you. No matter what, you'll learn to keep pushing forward.

GOLDEN EGGS

- You are not your mind. It is a powerful instrument to be used to manifest the reality you choose.
- Feed your brain, your super-computer, with as much data as you can. Read books, attend seminars, and enroll in courses.
- This is your life, your journey, and no one else's. You only get one chance. Make it great!
- Desire is one of the keys to success. What are the desires that drive you?
- Write down your goals. Think about them all the time.
- Create a vision board with images of the things you want to manifest in your life: a house, cars, net worth, businesses, vacations, relationships, health, and so on.
- Get yourself into the right state as often as you can. Jump around, sing, dance, shout, take cold showers, and laugh.
- Happiness is not a thing or an event. It is a choice and a habit you create. Choose to be happy, because you can!

CHAPTER THREE

───────────────

TAKE ACTION

Perturbation is defined as "a disturbance of motion, course, arrangement, or state of equilibrium." I always think of a pot of water placed on a hot stove when I hear this word. For a while, nothing happens, until you turn up the heat, of course. Then, as the water's molecules get more and more agitated and the water begins to boil, it begins to turn to steam because it can no longer stay in a liquid state.

This same process can be applied to human behavior. When we become unhappy in a given situation, maybe in our present job or relationship or with our weight, we become more and more agitated. In a sense, our molecules become aggravated and stressed, and they begin to vibrate vigorously. We approach a threshold or a ceiling where we are about to change state (our lives), if we so choose.

People who are experiencing perturbation tend to do one of two things when they reach a point of peak agitation: they change their state, or they turn down the heat.

Almost all of us get uncomfortable in our lives at some point. Our proverbial molecules start to vibrate as we wake up every day to face the same tired routine. We yearn for something better and for something more. Each day, the heat rises.

We can go on like this for years, becoming more uncomfortable with each passing day, until the time comes to decide: are we going to change our state, thereby changing our lives, or are we going to turn down the heat and return to our inactive, pre-agitation state?

I see far too many people who turn down the heat because they're scared. Change is, by definition, uncomfortable. Rather than dealing with the discomfort of change by quitting their job and starting their own business, for example, they will return to their old state, even if they are miserable there, because there is comfort in what we know.

It's a temporary relief, though. If you don't address the source of the agitation, perturbation will start over soon enough, and you'll be right back in the same situation.

The people I've seen who've made the opposite choice

and changed their state never go back to their old way of life. Once they crash through that ceiling, they keep soaring to heights they never thought possible, because their whole reality has shifted.

For many years, I kept getting perturbed and then returning to my old state. I knew I was an unhappy camper who was uncomfortable with my life. I would become agitated and start moving toward something new. But every time I had the chance to make a profound change in my life, I backed away from it. I settled for temporary relief and felt OK for a while. Then the cycle would repeat itself.

It wasn't until I turned down the opportunity to spearhead US operations at the company I mentioned earlier and started buying properties with Norm that I experienced the life-changing power of *not* turning down the heat.

If you don't push through the transformative phase of perturbation, you'll remain stuck and unhappy. I'm here to tell you that to get to the level of wealth you want, you're going to experience some scary change. Your next iteration produces a beautiful feeling when you're on the other side of change, but it's damn uncomfortable while you go through it.

If you want to be wealthy, you must become comfortable with being uncomfortable.

FEAR IS THE ENEMY OF CHANGE

So, what holds people back when they reach that boiling point? We've talked about it a little bit already. The primary obstacle for anyone trying to change their life is fear.

Fear of making the wrong decision. Fear of the unknown. Fear of a future worse than your current life. Even fear of success. The weird part is that even if someone is completely miserable, they're still afraid a change might make their life worse. It's absurd, but it's human nature.

Shouldn't we be more afraid of remaining in our misery than possibly changing our lives for the better? Life is way too short and precious to accept the status quo. Tony Robbins helped me understand this point when I heard him say at a seminar, "Don't tolerate good. Go for great." Yet most of us tolerate misery.

You don't have to accept unhappiness! Change might seem scary because it pushes us into the unknown, but "scary" doesn't mean "worse." Even if the change you make seems like a mistake at the outset, you can always course correct and push forward. If you continue down the path of positive change, eventually you will reach your objective.

Remember that fear emerges from the survival part of our brain (reptilian complex, lizard brain, or medulla) that wants to keep us safe, not see us change and succeed. That's why we must keep working on our mindset and turn off the messages that say *I'm not good enough, I'm going to fail*, or *I'll lose everything*. These thoughts come from the part of our brain that was helpful thousands of years ago when humans were fighting for survival. In the twenty-first century, they're counterproductive.

On the other hand, we can't simply switch off our fear response. Anybody who claims that you can become fearless doesn't understand fear. We can all experience fear at a moment's notice. The key is managing fear, which you can do through skill and self-control. With practice, you can begin to recognize fear and set it aside if it doesn't serve you.

One of the ways I like to help people deal with fear is to take them skydiving. The amount of fear—or "mind friction"—they experience during the hour before they jump is incredible. Up there, their mind comes up with every permutation of what can go wrong: *The airplane will fail, my parachute won't open, or my tandem partner will lose consciousness. If I die doing this, what will happen to my family?* Their mind never stops chattering.

As we get ready to jump, they're usually so nervous they're shaking. If I offered them a chance to return to the ground, I know most of them would take it.

Then the jump happens. Their face, once white with terror, transforms into the image of pure joy: smiles, wide-eyed exhilaration, and screams of happiness. When we land, they're on a high you only get when you've done something as crazy as jumping out of a plane. They're grinning from ear to ear and usually admit skydiving is the most fun they've ever had.

Had they let their fear steer the ship, they'd have robbed themselves of that joy.

Fear takes people out when they're on the precipice of something great, whether it's buying their first building, starting their own business, partnering with somebody, having their first baby, or committing to a new relationship. Moving ahead despite fear can lead you down the path to success. If you never act, you'll never discover the possibilities.

WAYS TO CONFRONT AND OVERCOME FEAR

Managing fear starts with awareness. Recognize where fear comes from, and be thankful for it. I mean that literally. Listen to the scared voice in your head giving you all the reasons you can't do something. Acknowledge the voice, say "thank you," and move on.

Time and again, I've seen people in situations where

they were afraid, and then once they broke through the fear, they experienced joy and exhilaration. It might have been night swimming in a lake, skydiving, or bungee jumping. They experienced great trepidation or anxiety leading up to the experience, then pure pleasure afterwards.

Fear is crucial to the process of change. In fact, if you're not fearful when making a massive change, I have to wonder if you're actually changing anything significant. Again, fear is natural. Sometimes, overcoming it can be as simple as jumping out of a plane.

I'm a huge proponent of putting yourself in situations that push you to the maximum.

Aside from jumping out of a perfectly good plane, I've swallowed fire, walked on glass, walked on fire, had a cement block broken on my chest while lying on a bed of nails, bent a five-foot piece of rebar with my neck, and bungee jumped. I did all of these in order to learn how to manage my fear and stretch my limits.

I wanted to experience the challenge of being extremely uncomfortable and then breaking through the barrier to the other side. Enlightened Warrior Training Camp, created by T. Harv Eker, really helped me in this regard. It's a fabulous five-day seminar experience that radically stretches your boundaries and shifts your ability to deal with fear.

The training was transformative for me and my partner, Norm, as we were both dealing with feelings of fear and limitation that needed to be addressed. I encourage you to find these kinds of experiences that test your fear and push you to the limit.

Doing things that are far outside your comfort zone will make you adept at handling fear. Public speaking is one of the top fears Americans have, even more so than death!

If you're looking for an opportunity to push past fear and discomfort, I recommend you put yourself in front of a group of people and speak to them about something— your passion, career, or life or any story that you want to share. When you finish, you'll have a euphoric sense of pride and accomplishment and want to do it again. It's why motivational speakers and musical artists love their job—performing gives you a one-of-a-kind rush.

Take anything in life that you're afraid of doing and commit to doing it. Choosing to take the plunge and challenge yourself is a healthy and highly rewarding process.

MANAGING FEAR

A simple exercise I learned in India is to bring your attention to the mid-frontal cortex. Imagine a bright light emanating from the base of your neck, where the lizard brain resides. Then, with your eyes closed, slowly bring that light to the area of the head just above the forehead. This is the mid-frontal cortex, where most creative thinking occurs. Take a few deep breaths while focusing on that area of your brain. You should feel a warm, positive sensation, almost a feeling of euphoria. This is the place from which decisions should emanate.

Observe the voices in your head (mind friction) affecting your ability to move forward. Notice that most of what the voices are professing is bullcrap. Remember: your ego does not want you to change and grow. The voices that attempt to take you out come from the ego's need to stay exactly where it is, even if it means staying miserable.

Get comfortable being UNcomfortable! Choose to act in spite of fear.

SURROUND YOURSELF WITH THE RIGHT PEOPLE

Up to this point, we've focused on self-improvement in preparation for action. You can't conquer the world with a faulty money mindset, limiting thoughts, or unchecked fear.

Once you're ready for the next action step, it's time to surround yourself with people who can support you during your wealth journey. As you go through perturbation and begin down this path of radical change, you need positive reinforcement, not naysayers.

Almost everybody around me was a naysayer when I decided to write my first book. I heard every kind of negative pronouncement to discourage me from writing it: *you're an amateur, you're not qualified to write a book, it'll never get published*, and on and on.

I always pushed back with examples of authors who did exactly what I was trying to do, but the truth is negative people don't want their viewpoint changed. They enjoy negativity. It's like a drug to them, which is why you shouldn't waste your time on them.

We are all the total of the five people we spend the most time with, so we need to surround ourselves with people who can help shape us into the person we want to become.

If you're trying to grow financially, you'd be wise to surround yourself with go-getters and people who are on a similar upward trajectory, if not already where you want to be. Your road will be smoother when you hang out with people who have already succeeded or who are trying to succeed.

It's not your job, and doesn't get you anywhere, to hang out with people who are negative in all the ways possible: naysayers, whiners, complainers, blamers, haters, critics, tear-downers. Even if you call them friends, they can hold you back from living the life of your dreams. It can be difficult to get away from them, because on some level, they want to attach themselves to your ambition yet don't want you to move forward.

If your growth and success mean you're going to separate from them, they don't want that. Whether consciously or subconsciously, they will try to take you out. Exactly like the old, negative belief-system voices in your head, those people will undermine you. They want you miserable with them, not happy in your success.

Get away from these people. It's not easy, and it can feel sad, but you need to do it. If it's someone who has been an important friend, then you can try and talk to them about it, urge them to change their outlook and their life, and encourage them to move forward with you.

But if they can't or won't change their outlook, then you need to move on.

I encourage you to join networking and mastermind groups in your city. You can also find like-minded people in professional organizations, on social media, or in online forums.

Get together once a week just to chat about positive things, growth, becoming millionaires, being happy, doing good in the world, and helping people. What you'll find is that being among amazing, positive people is nourishing for the soul.

Sometimes, I put together dinners, and I am incredibly selective about my guests. I might invite eight people, and they need to be very high-level in terms of positivity. I have lots of friends and many relatives, but these dinners are not a social free-for-all. I want to gather a small, select group who will all contribute to the energy and atmosphere I want.

As a result, the energy at these dinners flies high. It's fun and exciting, we laugh, and we talk about the world in a very positive way, whether it's about business or other topics. I serve good food, but the joy is through the chemistry of the people in that room.

If you're a young person, seek out groups at your school that align with your goals and are filled with positive people who will empower you, not tear you down. If you can't find one at your school, I know you can find one online. The aim here is to grow your skills and expand your knowledge base while also being filled with positivity.

You might also seek out a mentor—someone who has done what you're wanting to do and is willing to share their experiences and knowledge with you. This can be an adult or even someone your age. Age isn't important; what matters is developing a relationship in which both parties can benefit. You can learn from the experiences of the mentor, and the mentor can feel good knowing their wisdom is helping create another success story.

DEVELOP THE HABIT OF TAKING ACTION

I often see people who genuinely want to change their lives but don't because the thought of getting started feels so overwhelming. You want to develop the habit of taking action, and the best way to do that is to start small. You don't have to buy your first building right now, but you can start driving around your city and researching growing areas, striking up conversations with investors and developers, and crunching some numbers.

If you create good habits early, you'll be rewarded with results that grow.

You'll also be undaunted by larger challenges later if you choose to act. By starting small, you're maximizing your chances of success and minimizing the risk of failure. As you begin to stack up small victories, optimism and self-belief will blossom inside you.

For example, I bought a fifty-unit property. Soon after, I had an opportunity to buy a concrete elevator building with 160 units. Some people would just say, "Forget it—this is beyond my scope as an investor." I thought, "Wait a minute! I purchased a fifty-unit building and succeeded big time. A larger building shouldn't be much different, just a little more management and maybe another partner or investor. So I'll try!"

When you've done something before, taking it to the next level becomes easier.

There's an important step you can't skip before acting, however: do your homework. Crunch the numbers, in whatever sense that applies. Calculate the risk by diving into the research. Consult with your financial intuitions. See if the numbers make sense and if you believe in your gut that moving forward is the right decision. You can always choose to move forward when you don't feel entirely comfortable, but the more information you have, the better your decision and the less the risk.

You will make mistakes, but you'll learn, adjust, and move forward again.

I came out of university hoping to find a decent job and earn a living. That was going to be my life, and I was not at all happy with that reality. Making a million dollars was a pipe dream. In the four decades since then, mostly in the past few years, I've changed, grown, and taken plenty of risks. Now, I'm sitting here with a net worth that's hundreds of times larger than I ever could have dreamed.

Anyone can do what I did, but not many will, because it requires relentless action. I got knocked back a few times; however, I always got up and kept moving forward.

You don't need to be perfect starting out. You just need to take that first step.

SCHOOL IS AN IMPORTANT PART OF YOUR JOURNEY

One thing I don't want young people to take from this book is the false idea that school is pointless. I want to fill in the gaps where your school doesn't teach you about your mind and building wealth, but to fill in the gaps, you still need a foundation on which to build.

School is essential for shaping your brain into a tool that can be used to manifest the reality you want. It's not the be-all, end-all that society can make it out to be, but it is important for acquiring basic knowledge and developing skills you'll need to be successful. In fact, everything you learn in school enters your subconscious mind, your supercomputer, by osmosis and creates a great foundation for a productive database you can draw from.

I'm talking about university here as well. Many of the young people I speak with want to move straight into entrepreneurship when they graduate high school. I know a college degree doesn't always translate into financial success, but I do believe attending university affords you an incredible opportunity to improve your brain and ultimately your life.

If you study an area related to your passion, you'll discover new insights and develop new skills. Post-secondary education also trains you to deal with many challenges, including exams, seminars, presentations, essays, and pressure. The challenges of post-secondary education make you bigger, better, and more capable of handling life's challenges.

University is not the only path to success but rather another arrow in the quiver of a person's life. It can move you forward in a positive way if you parallel your efforts at school with acquiring financial information and taking small, calculated actions.

You can absolutely pursue your passion and build wealth at the same time. It's not an either/or proposition. I mentioned in the introduction that my son, Evan, wants to get into filmmaking. My advice to him was to build his wealth through real estate so he could finance his own movies. My daughter Sarah is still unsure of her direction, though she decided the sciences no longer hold her interest. She seems to like business and psychology. We'll see where she goes from here. My other daughter, Deanna, is still on the path toward medicine. In fact, she's wanted to be a pediatrician since she was six years old. Both of my daughters should pay heed to my guidance.

Parallel your pathway to a career with a wealth-building machine that will ultimately provide you with the freedom you yearn for. You don't have to be a full-time investor like I am. You can use what you learn at university to draw closer to your dream career and use what you learn in this book and elsewhere to build the kind of wealth that supports your passion.

Before we get into the specifics of wealth creation through my C.R.E.A.T.E.™ Formula, we need to cover some financial basics in the next couple chapters. I want you to be able to take full advantage of this formula, and to do that, there are a few things you need to understand.

GOLDEN EGGS
- No change can take place without taking action.

- Break through the ceiling of perturbation. You will never go back.
- Get comfortable being UNcomfortable. Change and growth is uncomfortable.
- Fear limits you and holds you back. Learn to manage fear. Stretch your boundaries. Act in spite of fear!
- Stretch your boundaries by doing things that scare you. How about skydiving, walking on hot coals, or speaking in public?
- Avoid the naysayers. Hang out with positive, like-minded people looking to grow and achieve success.
- Take action by starting with small steps. Instill the habit of executing. Ready, aim, FIRE!
- School adds to your subconscious supercomputer. It gives you extra tools, insights, and skills in order to grow. Augment your education by reading, attending seminars, and learning from successful people.

CHAPTER FOUR

MASTER THE BASICS

If you bring home a paycheck, have you ever stopped to look at how much you're actually bringing home and how much of each check gets eaten up by deductions? If you're a young person working a real job for the first time, this will be an eye-opening exercise for you.

When I began my career, I received a check with taxes already deducted from my gross pay (the amount before deductions). The government taxed my employer, and then it taxed me. Yikes, the government is seriously money hungry, and it will gouge you at every turn. Actually, multiple levels of taxes were taken from my gross pay.

In Canada, you have provincial and federal taxes. In the United States, you have federal, state, and local taxes. In addition to taxes, you will also have deductions for healthcare and retirement if your employer provides you with those perks.

When I started to look at the net amount (how much I made after deductions), it shocked me, because a huge percentage of my income got sliced off before I ever got paid.

What I brought home with each paycheck went toward my day-to-day living expenses. Once that money was spoken for or spent, close to zero remained to invest or try to build future wealth. This is how most people live: paycheck to paycheck, with no eye toward the future. They're merely trying to provide for their family and pay the bills.

Wealthy people, on the other hand, don't pay taxes off the top. (We'll cover this in Chapter Nine.)

You need to understand that tax laws were created for, and favor, business owners and investors. Tax laws don't favor employees. The majority of taxes collected in the United States, Canada, and other countries come from people who work for others.

This doesn't mean employees can't build wealth while supporting their quality of life. It simply means it's a much harder task for them. As I stated in the introduction, the difference between making $50,000 a year and $1 million a year is awareness.

It's difficult to be financially free if you don't understand the system, which starts with seeing the deductions from your paycheck and then creating a plan for what's left over.

Instead of spending your entire paycheck, put away 10 percent for investments. At the same time, put aside 5 to 10 percent for fun with your family and friends. You need balance in life, but it needs to be structured, and you must follow through with discipline.

The goal is to shift your relationship with money. Employees, self-employed individuals, and contractors work for money by the hour, which means there's a limit to how much they can make due to time constraints and how much they can charge. As we know, the wealthy among us make money while they sleep, and there's no limit to how much they can make.

By using your money to invest or start a business that can make money for you without your involvement and without limitations, you're moving toward financial freedom—that sweet spot where you have enough passive income to cover your lifestyle.

AVOID MAKING SUBPAR INVESTING DECISIONS

No matter your employment situation, you can begin building wealth with the money you have left over after paying your bills. It doesn't matter if it's five dollars or $5,000.

The problem is that many people make subpar choices when deciding how to invest their money, choosing flawed routes like savings accounts and mutual funds. I'm not saying you're wrong to invest by these means, just that there are better options out there.

Let's start with savings accounts. If you look at the banking system, interest rates on these accounts are minuscule. We've been in a low-interest environment for many years.

Money in a savings account will earn about 1 percent, and it's going to take a long time—too long—to build any wealth. One of the reasons your return is low in a savings account is because it's a safe bet. The banking system is unlikely to collapse. Your money will be there no matter what, but at 1 percent interest, it's barely growing at all. Compared to other ways to build wealth, money left in a savings account is commensurate to losing money.

It's fine to keep money in a savings account if you want to avoid spending it. Just don't choose that method as your primary means of building wealth (because you won't).

A mutual fund is an amalgamation of bonds and/or stocks of various companies that is controlled by a group of managers. Mutual funds can range from small (five companies) to large (hundreds of companies). If the managers are good at their job, the fund will perform well and give back a good return to the investor. Even though some of the stocks may not rise, the hope is that, as a group, the fund will rise in value over the long term.

The problem with mutual funds (both in the United States and Canada) is that the stocks being used in the funds are over-diversified and the exorbitant fees lower the rate of return. When the fees are too high, the fund needs to perform over and above the high percentage of fees that sometimes exceed 3 percent. Over a couple decades, we could be talking hundreds of thousands of dollars, depending on your initial investment.

Should there be fees? Yes, but with the right funds, fees shouldn't be much higher than 1 percent. But most mutual funds charge 2 to 3 percent in fees. As a result, these funds must perform at a level where they not only cover their fees but also give you a return!

How can they do that? I can tell you right now: most funds don't deliver. Many lose money, and after those fees, your growth will be extremely slow.

Alternatively, investing in index funds is a better bet.

They just follow the markets (depending on which one you invest in), and the fees are minimal.

BE CAREFUL WITH FINANCIAL ADVISORS

If you're using a financial advisor, let me offer a word of caution: don't hand the ball off to them entirely. A financial advisor should never be a substitute for learning the subject yourself. It's dangerous to blindly trust any financial advisor with your money.

When I sit down with a potential advisor, one of the first questions I ask them is "Are you a millionaire?" If they recommend a particular fund, I ask, "How much money did you make investing your own dollars into these funds that you're recommending?"

I ask them those questions because most financial advisors are just salespeople pushing products for their company. Their allegiances lie with the people signing their paycheck, not with you. That's not to say they're bad people who will light your money on fire with poor investments, just that they're not always looking out for your best interests.

Some financial advisors are successful for their clients, but they're few and far between. Furthermore, if you're dealing with the product-pushing salesperson or the rare successful professional, you can't avoid the problem of fees. The dirty little secret of the investing world is that executives and financial advisors make a profit even when you lose money.

When the market crashed in 2008, millions of hardworking people watched in horror as the wealth and savings they'd built over decades disappeared. Meanwhile, Wall Street executives walked away richer than ever. It was sickening. Many of these crooks should have gone to jail, yet their money and status protected them. Ten years later, I see people are falling back into the same traps due to a pervasive lack of understanding about money.

DON'T DABBLE IN THE STOCK MARKET

If savings accounts and mutual funds are flawed, how should you invest your money? For mid- to long-term wealth building, we'll talk about real estate in the coming chapters.

For short-term investment, I like dividend-oriented stocks with major companies whose histories go back decades. What that means is I'm buying a small ownership share in these companies, and when they make money, I get paid a dividend every so often (usually quarterly) that is equivalent to the size of my ownership share.

I only invest in solid companies worth billions of dollars

that have long histories of being profitable and a clear path forward for growth. I advise you to do the same. If you do a Google search for "companies that give dividends on the New York Stock Exchange" (or NASDAQ or other stock exchanges), you'll see a list of companies that pay dividends. But even with these dividend-paying stocks, there is risk your dividends will be wiped out when the stock goes down. And if the market were to crash, your stocks might plummet along with the market.

With all that said, don't dabble in the stock market. You'll very likely get burned.

I learned a painful lesson about stocks when I was in my early twenties and making good money. One day, a friend urgently recommended a stock to me that he was convinced was about to fly. I invested in it with no background information or knowledge of how the stock market worked. I simply trusted my friend and believed I was about to be rich.

After that, I fell into the trap of investing in a stock every time I got a tip. Like many people, playing in the stock market fed my need for instant gratification. Who has time for research and preparation when there are millions of dollars to be made, right?

I proceeded to lose a huge amount of money, and it was

entirely my fault. I was naïve, I didn't have anyone to help guide me, and I willfully chose not to educate myself.

I went for almost every stock tip that came my way without realizing that when Joe Public is getting information from a taxi driver about this stock that's about to rise, it's usually because the insiders have driven it up and are getting their money out.

When I finally pulled the plug, I owed the bank a lot of money—so much, in fact, that many people recommended I declare bankruptcy in order to wipe away the debt. I didn't go that route, choosing instead to slowly repay the debt down to the last penny.

Yes, there is money to be made in the stock market. I have a friend who is an options trader, but he has studied, has read a plethora of books, and is highly skilled. He has taken courses, practiced endlessly, and been tested. He makes money with stocks due to a massive foundational effort on his part.

On the other side of the spectrum, I have another friend in his sixties who had struggled financially his whole life. His mother died, and he inherited around $100,000. If he had invested it properly, the money might have finally given him a decent level of financial freedom. Instead, he put it into the stock market and lost more than 90 percent of it.

You cannot jump into the stock market thinking that you'll make big bucks based on a tip or some financial news article or TV segment. If you aren't educated and experienced, it's nothing more than a casino, and you know what happens in the casino.

LIQUIDITY IS VALUABLE WHEN INVESTING

An important concept in investing is liquidity, or how easily you can access your money.

In Canada, we can park our money in a short-term GIC (Guaranteed Investment Certificate) instead of a savings account. With this type of account, you deposit money for a set period of thirty to 364 days at a fixed interest rate. The longer your term, the higher the rate you generally earn. It's a safe place to park your money for a short period of time, while enjoying a guaranteed rate of interest and fully protected principal.

In the United States, the equivalent is known as a certificate of deposit, or a CD.

To know whether a GIC/CD is the right choice over a savings account, consider your liquidity needs. With a savings account, you can take money out at any time with no penalty. That's why the interest rate is so low: it carries no risk, and your liquidity is high.

If you're invested in a GIC/CD or mutual fund, though, you might be in trouble if you need to pull cash out for another investment. If you can pull money out early, you might have to pay a fee. A higher rate of return usually decreases the liquidity of your investment.

Stocks present a different challenge when it comes to liquidity. Imagine you invested in a stock, and in the short run, that stock decreased in value. Suddenly you find a piece of real estate that you want to buy and need money for the down payment.

Now you're facing a difficult choice: sell the stock at a loss to get the cash you need, or hold the stock and hope for increased value, possibly at the expense of your real estate deal.

You see now why it's important to carefully consider your liquidity needs?

That's why I said earlier that a savings account earning 1 percent interest is not the worst idea in the world. If you need liquid funds, it can be a means to an end.

LOOK FOR CREATIVE WAYS TO INVEST

Another way of looking at wealth building is through something called *iterations*. My business partner, Norm, is an analytical thinker when it comes to making money. One time, he showed me an iteration worksheet he created. It exhibited how, with a small investment, he could build wealth through iterations. What that means is that by doubling his money with every decision, or at least procuring a high return on each of his investments, he could incrementally increase his net worth.

Norm swore by these iteration worksheets, and he began his investing by purchasing $10,000 worth of computer paper being liquidated by Staples. He knew the market for computer paper, and he also knew he was buying it for pennies on the dollar.

He sold that paper quickly and doubled his profit.

I love this example because it shows what you can do if you research a particular market and make a smart, calculated move. Norm knew that paper was being sold cheap, and he knew that he would be able to resell it at a much higher price.

If you make a move where you can double or triple your money, and if the risk is almost nothing, then this is a great early move when your funds are low.

HARNESS THE POWER OF COMPOUNDING

Whatever investment you make, remember that Albert Einstein once called compound interest the most powerful force in the universe. He also said, "Compound interest is the eighth wonder of the world. He who understands it, earns it. He who doesn't, pays it." That was a genius talking. Shouldn't we all pay heed?

We'll cover compounding in the next chapter, but here's a quick demonstration. If you don't fully understand compound interest, this should whet your appetite for what's to come.

Imagine the interest rate on an investment you make is 10 percent. In a compound-interest investment, that 10 percent interest after the first year goes back into your investment, which has now increased by 10 percent without you lifting a finger.

If you originally put in $1,000, you now have $1,100 after one year. That one hundred dollars in interest you earned immediately starts working for you because over the next year, instead of earning 10 percent on $1,000, you're now earning that rate of return on $1,100.

So instead of earning one hundred dollars in interest, you will earn $110 after the second year.

This process continues year after year, turning your initial $1,000 into $117,390.58 after fifty years. Isn't that amazing? With compounding, you create money like magic!

Another example of the power of compounding: which would you choose, a penny doubling every day for thirty-one days or a check for $5 million?

Well, if you chose the check for $5 million, you would have given up over $5 million! That's right—doubling a penny for thirty-one days would give you over $10,737,000!

Now that you understand the importance of the mind in building wealth and have a handle on some financial basics, you're ready to jump into the next chapter and look at the "C" in the C.R.E.A.T.E.™ Formula: compounding. Are you ready? Let's do it!

GOLDEN EGGS

- Make smart investment decisions. Today's decisions can lead to tomorrow's pain or triumphs.
- Mutual funds are not what you think they are. Beware.
- Choose your financial advisors carefully. Most are just paper-pushing salespeople.
- The stock market is a casino for those who are not fully trained. Don't dabble in this dangerous place. Immerse yourself fully or avoid it.

- Cash is king. Having liquidity within your investments can help you move fast on deals that come your way.
- Fully connect with the power of compound interest or the compounding effect. It is your friend when it comes to building wealth.
- As Albert Einstein said, "Compound interest is the eighth wonder of the world. He who understands it, earns it. He who doesn't, pays it."

CHAPTER FIVE

COMPOUND
YOUR MONEY

To begin this chapter, I'd like you to take a close look at where your money goes.

First, look at what you're spending on extras. Extras could be anything from fancy clothes to eating out at nice restaurants to buying expensive cars. We all need to treat ourselves from time to time, but extravagant expenses sabotage your ability to build wealth.

If you're twenty years old and spending indiscriminately, I want to show you what can happen if you put that money away and let it grow for you. It's not an exaggeration to say that over twenty or thirty years (which seems far away but really isn't), your initial sum of money could grow to well over a million dollars thanks to compounding.

Don't believe me? Here's a story from one of my previous books that I wanted to share here. I'm still kicking myself for the spending habits I had when I was young. When you see the sum of money I could be sitting with today, it'll blow your mind.

WHAT COULD HAVE BEEN

Several years ago, I was going through my closet and dresser, getting rid of rarely worn clothes and shoes. My closet and drawers were packed tight, and I had no room for anything. I tossed the old shirts, pants, suits, and shoes into a pile on my bed that slowly got bigger and bigger. As I gazed at the rapidly growing pile of clothing and footwear—most of which was premium quality and much of which I rarely wore—I had an epiphany.

I began to think about the sheer amount of hard-earned cash I had spent over the years on this mountain of rejects. Many of the clothes and shoes were at least a decade old.

I picked up a shirt that I had paid more than one hundred dollars for at Ralph's Men's Store. There was a pullover that cost seventy-five dollars, a ninety-five-dollar pair of corduroys, and a $150 Robert Graham shirt. I found a pair of beige leather shoes that cost $150, yet I never wore them, because they pinched my heel. Four suits, each more than $400, hadn't fit me for over ten years!

I went through the pile and did the math. These rejects had cost me $17,500 over the years!

My mind raced as I considered what $17,500 would be worth today if I had invested it instead of blowing it on extra clothes. I knew in my gut that the results would be terrible.

For this exercise, I assumed a 10 percent rate of return. With banks, that's a high rate, but in my world of real estate investing, 10 percent is very easily achieved.

If I had taken the $17,500 and earned 10 percent annually, I would have doubled my money in ten years without reinvesting the 10 percent return I made each year. Now, let's tap into the power of compounding. Had I put the 10 percent annual return back into my initial investment each year, I would have made $45,390 instead of $35,000.

Instead of a worthless pile of clothes, after ten years, I could have been sitting with $45,390 to invest. And after twenty years, I could have enjoyed $117,729!

The simple math of my wasteful consumerism motivated

me to check out other rooms of my house. I repeated the exercise with several boxes of old or unused electronics. I was amazed by the calculators, adding machines, cell phones, adapters, speakers, and wires that I had accumulated. I estimated the worth of the useless equipment to be $15,000.

I found boxes of CDs and DVDs. Did I really need all the CDs? I rarely listened to them, and if I did, I listened to most only once. It was even worse with the DVDs. I had tons of them and had only ever watched them one time. Suddenly, all of this ownership made no sense.

I had a $1,500 laser-disc player and collection of laser discs, all for a technology fad that only lasted a year! Then, I found video games, consoles, and controllers that had become obsolete as newer games and equipment emerged. I calculated that I'd spent $20,000 for all my various entertainment equipment and technology over the years.

Another area of waste was furniture. I couldn't believe how many pieces I'd purchased over the years that lost two-thirds of their value the minute they left the store. I could have saved money by purchasing well-made antiques rather than trendy, cheap items. It was hard to calculate the exact amount of waste, but I estimated it at about $50,000.

I decided not to revisit the amount of money wasted on various cars through the years, or the money I'd lost in the stock market (as you'll recall from the last chapter).

Between the clothes ($17,500), old electronics ($15,000), entertainment items ($20,000), and furniture ($50,000), the total amount of money wasted came to approximately $102,500.

That sum, invested at 10 percent and compounded over ten years, came to a total of $265,858. After twenty years, that number would have grown to $689,567!

How many of you would like to be sitting with a quarter of a million dollars in your bank account right now? How about almost three-quarters of a million? And this is only based on frivolous expenditures! You can do the calculations based on your financial reality and spending habits to see how much money you could have in ten or twenty years.

Let's take it a step further with my numbers. What if I had gotten a 20 percent annual return, which is the very minimum I received with my real estate investments? After ten years, my money would have grown to over $634,000. After twenty years, my money would have grown to $3,925,560!

At a 30 percent rate of return, my money would have grown to over $1.4 million in ten years.

What if my money were working for twenty years instead of only ten and at a 30 percent interest rate? And what if I included the money I'd wasted on the myriad of cars, car stereos, spoilers, and more? Well, I will avoid the pain of this gigantic retirement-level number and move on.

So, the next time you're shopping for a new shirt, laptop, or piece of furniture, I implore you to consider what could be, with better choices and compound interest.

GOOD DEBT VS. BAD DEBT

In the same way investments can grow rapidly through compounding, so can debt. If you're a young person who has money to spend for the first time, you need to be aware of what I call "good debt" versus "bad debt" before you begin your wealth-building journey.

As I've said previously, it's fine to have fun when you're young. You should allot 5 to 10 percent of your income to date nights, vacations, or new clothes.

Where most young people get in trouble is that, over time, they let the pervasive influence of consumerism overwhelm whatever financial discipline they've built up.

We're programmed by credit card companies to spend far beyond our means on things we don't need. Credit card debt is out of control now, and credit card companies relentlessly push and promote their product. Companies even make phone calls to people to offer increased credit limits so that they're encouraged to spend more money. Many people accept the increased limits, then blow the money without a second thought.

When it comes time to pay off the balance, they're content paying the minimum and get subjected to the credit card company's extremely high interest rates. What started as a small debt will continue to snowball through a twisted kind of compounding.

Credit card debt is an example of bad debt that causes untold social problems: divorce, bankruptcies, stress-related illnesses, even suicides. Debt is not just about money.

An example of good debt is a mortgage you take out to buy an apartment building. Unlike bad debt, which takes money from you, good debt can put money in your pocket.

With a mortgage, you will owe banks or individuals money with interest, but it's good debt because your property will build your net worth. You'll repay the people and institutions from the proceeds of the property, and you'll own the property.

Credit cards aren't always used to rack up bad debt. Let me give you an example.

Imagine that you have the opportunity to buy a quadruplex. It's undervalued, the rents are low, and you're certain that it's a great deal. Maybe you're $20,000 short and you really need to make your move quickly, but you don't have an investor to help you.

If your current credit allows it, you can take the cash from your credit card to buy that property. That debt is now credit card debt, which is normally a bad thing; however, this property is going to earn hundreds of thousands of dollars, so it now becomes "good" debt.

Unlike most purchases, you've used your credit card to purchase an asset.

You can use the monthly cashflow from the building to pay off the balance on the card before the high interest rate has a chance to bury you in mounting debt.

BUYING MY FIRST BUILDING

Norm and I bought our first building in 2006. It was a forty-seven-unit building that cost us around $2 million. It was like our baby, and we got a crash course on property management with that building. We kept it rented, we kept it clean, and we managed it well.

After about a year, we contacted our bank because we needed some money for renovations. We asked the bank to lend us about $40,000. Our account manager said he'd look into it. He came back to us about a day later saying, "We looked at your file, and we looked at the building, and we can give you $600,000." We were confused.

He explained, "Your revenue is up and your expenses are streamlined. We can refinance your mortgage right now and give you $600,000." I looked at Norm. He looked at me. We were both in total shock. Of course, we accepted the increased mortgage, and because the higher building revenue covered our higher mortgage payments, we now had $600,000 to split between us. In Chapter Eight, you'll see how I spent my half. (*Hint*: not well.)

When you refinance a property like we did, what you can do with the money differs based on where you live. In Canada, you can take that money and pocket it, but at some point in the future, taxes must be paid. Either you die (and have a deemed disposition) or you sell.

In the United States, when you sell a property or pull money out from refinancing, you need to invest it into a new building to avoid paying taxes. This is called a 1031 Exchange.

Norm and I continued to take care of our baby, thereby increasing its value. Over the years, we refinanced a few more times and used that money to purchase other buildings.

From 2006 to 2016, we went from owning forty-seven units to almost 1,000. By doing so, we've increased the impact compounding has on our net worth twenty times over.

After twelve years, Norm and I decided to sell our forty-seven-unit building. We paid $2 million in 2006 and sold the building for $6 million in 2018.

If we were young men, we might have kept the building, but Norm and I are both over sixty now, and we want to speed up the velocity of money, which I'll explain later.

You might look at this story and say, "That's great Robert, but I don't have $2 million to buy my first building. How am I supposed to get started in real estate without money?"

As we'll see later in the book, you don't need your own money to get started with real estate investing. You can use banks, investors, partners, and OPM (other people's money).

Of course, if you have your own money, you'll make more money with each deal. But don't let this idea of "I need money to make money" stop you from pursuing real estate.

OTHER AVENUES FOR INVESTING

As you can see, real estate is a reliable avenue for investing. We bought one building with forty-seven units, took care of it, and sold it twelve years later for a $4 million profit.

We laid out some short-term investing options in the last chapter, but there are other long-term investing avenues besides real estate—for example, option trading (stocks). Again, do not dabble in this sometimes-dangerous area.

You can buy oil wells, although I don't recommend that for young people. As with any investment you make, you really need to know your stuff. Of course, these are skills you can learn and knowledge you can certainly obtain.

A better option might be investing in startup companies. The same guidelines that applied with buying stock apply here: look for solid companies with technologies that have a clear growth path and a superb management and operations team. Education is critical. If you dabble, you're more likely to get burned. The numbers are clear: only about 10 percent of startups make it.

I'll never forget about twenty years ago when people were investing during the dot-com boom. I was involved with a company that had a valuation of $80 million before it even went public (began selling stock). We had an amazing board of directors, and we were about to enter the market, which would have made us all a fortune.

But the dot-com bubble burst before we could go public, and the company's value evaporated overnight.

Technology is more stable today in terms of investing, but with the rapid advancements being made every day, the difference between cutting edge and obsolete can be weeks.

That's why I hang my hat on real estate. People won't always use certain technologies, and we're slowly moving away from fossil fuels, but people will always need a place to live. Through ups, downs, and corrections, real estate values always go up in the long run.

That's why I encourage people, no matter what investments they make, to own at least one building.

If you're building a startup company, good for you. I love that. Building a company and making a lot of money is an exciting thing. But I also strongly encourage you to own a piece of real estate or two, because that real estate will grow. No matter what happens with your startup, your other investments, or your career, that real estate will take care of you. It may take care of you, your family, and, if you're smart enough, the generations to come.

TAKE ADVANTAGE OF COMPOUNDING NOW

I've been able to accomplish a lot financially since my late forties. That said, I often stop and ask myself, "What if? What if someone had taught me this in my late teens or early twenties? Where would I be today if I had started decades earlier?"

With compounding, time is the secret ingredient. If you get started in your late teens or early twenties, your time horizon can be much longer than mine was at forty-seven.

With a longer time horizon comes the possibility of a much higher return. Take a look at this chart to see the power of investing at twenty, thirty, and forty.

COMPOUNDING INTEREST TIME HORIZON

Age	Initial Investment		-
	100,000	200,000	200,000
	Annual Return		
	10%	20%	30%
20	$ 110,000	$ 240,000	$ 260,000
21	$ 121,000	$ 288,000	$ 338,000
22	$ 133,100	$ 345,600	$ 439,400
23	$ 146,410	$ 414,720	$ 571,220
24	$ 161,051	$ 497,664	$ 742,586
25	$ 177,156	$ 597,197	$ 965,362
26	$ 194,872	$ 716,636	$ 1,254,970
27	$ 214,359	$ 859,963	$ 1,631,461
28	$ 235,795	$ 1,031,956	$ 2,120,900
29	$ 259,374	$ 1,238,347	$ 2,757,170
30	$ 285,312	$ 1,486,017	$ 3,584,321
31	$ 313,843	$ 1,783,220	$ 4,659,617
32	$ 345,227	$ 2,139,864	$ 6,057,502
33	$ 379,750	$ 2,567,837	$ 7,874,753
34	$ 417,725	$ 3,081,404	$ 10,237,179
35	$ 459,497	$ 3,697,685	$ 13,308,332
36	$ 505,447	$ 4,437,222	$ 17,300,832
37	$ 555,992	$ 5,324,667	$ 22,491,081
38	$ 611,591	$ 6,389,600	$ 29,238,406
39	$ 672,750	$ 7,667,520	$ 38,009,928
40	$ 740,025	$ 9,201,024	$ 49,412,906
41	$ 814,027	$ 11,041,229	$ 64,236,778
42	$ 895,430	$ 13,249,475	$ 83,507,811
43	$ 984,973	$ 15,899,369	$ 108,560,154
44	$ 1,083,471	$ 19,079,243	$ 141,128,200
45	$ 1,191,818	$ 22,895,092	$ 183,466,660
46	$ 1,310,999	$ 27,474,110	$ 238,506,659
47	$ 1,442,099	$ 32,968,932	$ 310,058,656
48	$ 1,586,309	$ 39,562,719	$ 403,076,253
49	$ 1,744,940	$ 47,475,263	$ 523,999,129
50	$ 1,919,434	$ 56,970,315	$ 681,198,867

In the example above, I used a simple formula to show you the power of compounding. With only one injection at the outset and without ever adding anything to the pie, just receiving a compounded return, I could make millions and millions of dollars over time. In my case, just by doing the same things I've been doing for the last fourteen years in real estate, but starting at twenty years old, I could be sitting with hundreds of millions of dollars right now. The value of time in this equation can't be overstated.

I'm writing this book for young people, so they get the information I never got.

Yes, your parents can turn their financial lives around by doing the things covered in this book. However, they won't be able to go as far as you, because they are limited by time. Their time horizon is thirty or forty years, whereas yours can be double that.

It's true there is no expiration date on success. It's also true there's no minimum age to start building wealth. If you have the drive to acquire knowledge, set goals, and use the steps in this book to buy your first building, you can start as early as you want.

For teenage readers and those in their early twenties, I'm not talking about making a million dollars. Making a million dollars is easy peasy. I'm talking about making tens of millions, if not hundreds of millions, of dollars. Does that sound good to you?

If so, let's jump into the "R" of the C.R.E.A.T.E.™ Formula: return on investment.

GOLDEN EGGS

- Learn the C.R.E.A.T.E.™ Formula, starting with compounding.
- Spend your money wisely. The video game or concert ticket you buy today could become a down payment for a car twenty years from now.
- Know the difference between "good debt" and "bad debt." Good debt leads to more money in your pockets. Bad debt leads to empty pockets.
- One building can become your golden goose for years to come. My first building made us $4 million plus all the cashflow I received for years.
- There are many ways to invest and build wealth. Real estate is my favorite by far. You can also build wealth through stocks, options, oil wells, self-storage, and much more. Know your industry very well. Don't dabble in any one of these. Focus!
- When starting young, the compounding effect becomes your biggest ally. When you have a thirty- or forty-year horizon, a strong mindset, and wealth-

building awareness, you can make hundreds of millions of dollars.

CHAPTER SIX

DIFFERENTIATE WEALTH FROM INCOME

I'll never forget the first time I walked out of a real estate closing with a six-figure check. I was young, and that amount of money seemed insane to me. In my mind, I was rich!

The first thing I did was call my father to tell him the news. Much to my surprise, he wasn't impressed. He said, "I don't care about your income, what did you make net? What do you have to show for it now?"

I remember those words because now I understand why he asked me that question.

Your income does not equal your net pay if you have taxes

and other deductions taken out. Along those same lines, a large income does not mean you have a high net worth.

I didn't understand those concepts when I was young and excited about a six-figure payday, but in the forty-plus years since those days, I've learned these truths by living them.

Think back to the introduction. When I set up the hypothetical scenario where you now had the income of a doctor or an attorney, if you're like most people, you thought, "I'm rich!"

We now know why that's not necessarily true. Many high-income individuals would be in financial trouble if they stopped receiving their paycheck. When you consider all the ways people lose their jobs nowadays—mass layoffs, corporate mergers, outsourcing, workplace accidents—you can see why income is not a reliable barometer of wealth.

Don't spend all your time focused on ways to increase your income. Instead, start looking at ways to grow your net worth by acquiring assets that will give you a high return on your investment. The younger you are when you make this mental shift, the better.

The other day, at a conference I was speaking at, I met a fifteen-year-old boy and his father. The young boy told me he had just purchased his first rental house. I was taken aback by this boy's age and his hunger to start his real estate journey at such a young age. I told him that I wouldn't doubt it if he purchased his first hundred-unit building in his mid-twenties. His response astounded me: "I will buy my first hundred-unit apartment building before I'm twenty!" Wow, his confidence at the age of fifteen excited me.

The lesson here is simple: you're never too young to begin building your fortune!

SHIFTING YOUR FOCUS TO YOUR NET WORTH

The first step to increasing your net worth is understanding what it means.

Here's a simple formula: *What You Own – What You Owe = Your Net Worth.*

Pay attention to the word "own" here. Many people think their house is an asset, but unless it's a rental, it's not an asset because it's taking money out of their pocket in the form of monthly mortgage payments, utilities, taxes, and maintenance. Even when a house is paid off, it only becomes an asset when it's sold, unless it's generating income by other means like renting out a bedroom or the entire property.

Remember: assets put money in your pocket.

I don't want you to think based on what I've said that income plays no role in your wealth-building journey. At the outset, when your funds are low, income is vital. I'll also reiterate here that the level of income is not as important as what you do with it.

I've seen people begin with measly salaries go on to create real net worth. They were able to do it by taking a disciplined, structured approach with their money and investments. It took some time, but they turned their income into a significant net worth.

If you're a teenager working your first summer job, or you're fresh out of college working in your first salaried position, you can begin working on your net worth right now.

As we discussed in previous chapters, start by taking 10 percent of your net pay and investing it. Even if it's just a savings account, you're developing the habit of setting money aside every month, which is more important at your age than a big return rate.

This isn't offhand advice; I tell my kids the same thing. My son, Evan, is now at university studying business, but in junior college he worked at the snack bar of a movie theater. He took a percentage of his paycheck each month and put it into an account he didn't touch. Yes, his monthly contributions were small, but he developed the habit of saving. My daughter Sarah is in junior college while working at a retail clothing store and as a model at the same time. She, too, has developed the habit of putting money away and is enjoying watching her bank account grow every week. Even my youngest daughter, Deanna, is saving her allowance and babysitting money, and slowly building her bank account.

If you know how to make an Excel spreadsheet, that's a great way to start tracking your net worth. Create columns for income, taxes, expenses, savings, and assets. Take a look at this example chart for a better idea of how to set up your spreadsheet.

NET WORTH

2019		Jan	Feb	Mar	Apr	May	Jun	Jul	Aug	Sep	Oct	Nov	Dec
Current Assets	Cash												
	Stocks/Mutual Funds												
	Savings												
	Term Deposits/GICs												
	RRSP/401K												
	Total Current Assets												
Fixed Assets	Home												
	Furniture												
	Car												
	Investment Properties*												
	Businesses												
	Total Fixed Assets												
	Total Assets (Current+Fixed)												
Current Liabilities	Credit Cards												
	Line of Credit												
	Short Term Loans												
	Outstanding Bills												
	Total Current Liabilities												
Long Term Liab.	Mortgages–Home												
	Mortgages–Investments*												
	Total Long Term Liabilities												
	Total Liab. (Current+Long Term)												
	NET WORTH (Assets – Liabilities)												

At the beginning, your income, savings, and assets will be small. Meanwhile, the spending and taxes categories will frustrate the hell out of you. Don't get discouraged. Over time, you'll see steady growth that will eventually become parabolic (take off like a rocket).

If your net worth is growing every week, month, and year, then you are on the right path, regardless of your income or career. Watching as your net worth is growing toward the first million mark is a great feeling. It will help you shift your thinking away from how much income you bring home to how many assets you own.

THE MINDSET THAT KEEPS US TRAPPED

If you have the mindset that security comes from a steady job and regular paycheck, you probably inherited that mindset from your parents. It's part of your money mindset. Your parents may have worked for the same company, or for the government, for decades. If that's what your parents believed was secure, you'll probably believe it, too.

That's why mastermind groups, networking events, and seminars are so important, especially for young people. These groups help us escape the limiting mindsets that rule our behavior and replace them with mindsets that empower us to pursue financial freedom.

I've talked a lot about awareness, but did you know that awareness and intelligence are different? You can be a smart person and still lack awareness. Many geniuses struggle financially because their brilliance doesn't translate to sound financial awareness and decision-making.

The expectation that you'll be employed indefinitely, and that a job will keep you secure, is irresponsible and risky. I believe it's less risky to go out and make a million dollars.

The concept of retirement most people have also needs to be reevaluated. People wonder, "Am I ever going to be able to retire? Will there ever be a time when I can relax after the hard work I've put into my life, raising my children, working like a dog?"

Pensions and social security—once two legs of the sturdy retirement "stool," along with personal savings—can't be relied upon to carry us in our golden years anymore. If you want to retire, you need enough passive income to cover your cost of living.

Norm and I like to call that "covering our nut." (Get your mind out of the gutter!) Covering our nut means taking care of our expenses with passive income.

To do that, I had to migrate from the left side of the Work Smart table to the right.

WORK SMART RULE

In the table below, you will see two separate approaches to money. On the left side of the table, you can see the WORK HARD approach to making money and the obstacles to building wealth. On the right side of the table, you can see the WORK SMART approach to making money and the catalysts to building wealth.

JOB/SELF-EMPLOYED	INVESTMENTS/MEDIUM-LARGE BUSINESS
WORK HARD (Live off a few eggs from someone else's Golden Goose)	**WORK SMART** (Create and build your own Golden Goose)
• Shackled to a **Job** • No income without you • Paid by the hour/week/year • Time-based rewards • Limited growth potential • Higher taxes • Little **Freedom** • Minute or no compounding effect	• Fast track to **Freedom** • Make money while you sleep or on vacation • Wealth-building platform • Money and/or system works *for* you • Lower and/or deferred taxes • Powerful compounding effect

MIGRATE

*Based on Robert Kiyosaki's Cashflow Quadrant™

It's quite simple. Those on the left or WORK HARD side of the table—in other words, those who have jobs or are self-employed (own a job)—work hard for their money and are fighting an uphill battle in their quest to build wealth. They are shackled to their job and will struggle to attain any freedom. They work long and hard for their money.

Those on the right or WORK SMART side of the table—in other words, those who own a medium to large business or they invest on a constant basis (or both)—make money while they sleep and have the freedom to create the life they dream. Money works for them!

It's very hard to build wealth on the left side, because you're paying higher taxes and facing restrictions with your time and earning potential. The way to accelerate the process of wealth building is to migrate over to the right side.

This doesn't mean you have to quit your job today and jump over to the other side. You certainly can—I did—but it's pretty scary. Becoming a business owner or investor is a process, but what's nice about real estate is that if you own and manage property through a corporation, like an LLC, you've got the whole right side covered.

You can be employed, receiving that paycheck, while at the same time working to migrate over to the right side. If you're on the left side, start planning and putting money away. Research new business ideas or investments you might want to make.

The goal is to create passive income that isn't tied to your time or efforts.

I have many friends who are working day jobs and came

to me for help because they wanted to purchase a small building on the side. I didn't tell them to quit their jobs. I advised them to look for a six- or eight-plex, find a partner, and buy their first building while remaining employed. Get a feel for the business, and take care of your baby.

Some of them, after they'd acquired a few properties, told me, "Wow, that's the fastest way to become a multimillionaire. I'm quitting my job and committing to real estate." What's beautiful about the WORK SMART RULE is that there are many ways to move from the left side to the right side. You can take the slow, steady approach like my friends did by owning property on the side. You can also throw yourself completely into an idea.

I've invested in a couple of startup companies now where the founders did exactly that. They came out of school with a hope and a dream. They worked on a plan, assembled their team, built a product, and went after investors. They have no safety net. In their mind, it's do or die with this business idea. I admire their entrepreneurial spirit.

If you're still in school, or you have a job and are making decent money to start, that's fine. There's nothing wrong with that. But you need to start thinking about migrating to the right side. You need to think about how you plan to build net worth. You don't want to end up struggling with debt and living paycheck to paycheck.

REAL ESTATE OFFERS A HIGH ROI

I've mentioned some of the reasons I like real estate as an investment category, but besides a passion for the industry, the biggest draw for me is that real estate provides a high return on investment (ROI). You may be able to find non-brick-and-mortar investments that will get you close to 10 percent, but good luck finding one that will produce the kind of results we accomplished (multimillions) in such a short time frame (twelve years) with so little risk.

Real estate is brick and mortar (or dirt and grass, if it's land). It's tangible. You can see it and touch it every day. Not only that, you can learn about it just by being around it.

Real estate is not complicated. You don't need a master's degree to understand it. In fact, I've met uneducated people who have made millions of dollars in real estate.

My father came from a family with six kids and no money. He had to leave school after sixth grade and go to work to help put food on the table, yet he got into real estate and built a multimillion-dollar business all on his own (with a little help, of course). I think he had a type of "unconscious competence." I'm not sure he understood everything I'm writing about in this book. To be honest, I truly believe my father wasn't really sure about the level of wealth he was building and how it was being created.

He just made some decisions, and they worked out. I give him all the credit in the world for taking action.

There are so many ways to earn a significant ROI with real estate. You have cashflow, which is the money coming your way every month from tenants who pay rent (minus expenses and mortgage payments).

Those rent payments will cover your mortgage and expenses, meaning you don't need a lot of money for a down payment. For a million-dollar building, you might only have to put down $100,000.

But guess what happens? You get a return on the full value of the property, not just on the money you invested. This is called leverage, and we'll discuss it more in just a moment.

As you pay off your mortgage, you increase your equity (equity buildup), which is the difference between the original mortgage amount and the mortgage balance owed to the lender at a given moment. If the property value is going up, your equity increases even faster.

When the value of your property increases, it's called appreciation. With rental property, appreciation can happen a couple different ways: you raise the rent and/or you lower your expenses (and therefore, you increase your cashflow and net operating income—to be discussed in the next chapter), or the market in your area improves. You can also employ forced appreciation, which is making improvements to the property that increase its value.

With my buildings, I create forced appreciation by installing a new awning or giving the building a name. These are both small ways you can raise the perception of a building's value to prospective and existing tenants. (We'll look at others in Chapter Eight.)

USING LEVERAGE TO YOUR ADVANTAGE

Leverage is the ability to buy more real estate with less money invested. The more real estate you can buy with the least amount of money, the more leverage you can create.

Knowing how much cash you'll need for a deal is important for a couple reasons. Obviously, you have to know how much you need to raise or how much of your own money you're going to use, but it also has an effect on the numbers. As a general rule, the higher your leverage—or the lower the amount of money needed to purchase it—the higher your return on investment. Of course, that return also depends on your interest rate.

If you can take your available cash and use just half of

it for one property, you can put the other half toward buying a second property, which creates further leverage, because now you're invested in two properties. The objective is to own as much real estate as possible, because that real estate is working for you twenty-four hours a day building wealth. The more of it that you own, the more millions you'll make in the long run.

It's true that you can put more cash down when purchasing property, which will make your mortgage payment smaller and thereby increase your monthly cashflow.

Here I would remind you of the income-versus-wealth debate we had earlier. When you buy real estate, you're not doing it to build cashflow; you're doing it to build wealth.

The magic is found in increasing your net operating income (more on this in the next chapter) so that the value of the property increases, which will make you millions of dollars over time. You cannot be overly focused on cashflow. Don't get me wrong: you want to manage your building well and keep a steady cashflow, but that's not your focus.

Keep in mind that cashflow is taxable as income. As we'll see in Chapter Nine, you can erase it with capital cost allowance (depreciation) so that you don't have to pay taxes in the short run, but at the end of the day, where's the wealth coming from? It's not coming from the cash-flow. It's coming from building the value of that property, which, in turn, affects your net worth.

If you have one building with big cashflow, and you have all your money and resources in that one building, the growth of your net worth will be limited by that one property.

Leverage is like a cheat code in the game of real estate. Being able to enjoy all the benefits we just discussed without having to cover the full cost of your investment is magical.

USING LEVERAGE TO BUY 160 UNITS

Let me show you how this works with an example from my portfolio.

Norm and I bought a 160-unit property for $14 million, which was more than we intended. The property had juice—meaning we saw great potential to increase the rents and its value—but the numbers weren't there yet from the bank's point of view, so we only got about $9.8 million (or 70 percent) financed. We had to cover the other 30 percent.

I negotiated hard with the seller for him to carry a second

mortgage (called a balance of sale or vendor take-back) of $3 million (about 21 percent) and give me a preferred interest rate of 2 percent. The seller would carry the balance of sale for three years, and because I negotiated well, we wouldn't pay interest until those three years were up.

We purchased a $14 million property with just $1.2 million cash down. The value of the property has already increased to $19 million in two years. We anticipate it will reach at least $21 million in value within the next year, at which point we might sell.

Before that, we might refinance the property and pull out a few million dollars to split between us. Best of all, thanks to Canadian law, any money we pull out will be tax-deferred, meaning we'd only pay taxes when we sell the building or when we pass away.

Buying 160 units for $1.2 million cash down, increasing the property's value by $5 million or more in two years, and being able to pull out a few million to split—now that is leverage!

EARNING THE HIGHEST POSSIBLE RETURN

Here's another example of using leverage that might make your head spin.

Let's say I buy a property with a first mortgage of 75 percent from the bank, a second mortgage with the owner of 10 percent (balance of sale), and 15 percent of my cash.

I'll receive a return on my 15 percent based on an amalgamation of cashflow, appreciation, equity buildup, and forced appreciation. After two years of owning the building, I've raised the rents and lowered the expenses, so I go to the bank to refinance the property.

By refinancing, I'm able to pull out enough cash to cover the 15 percent I put down (and maybe more). Now, my property is fully financed for the amount I bought it for two years earlier.

For the math nerds out there, what's my return now that I have no cash in the deal?

That's right: it's infinite (since you can't divide into zero).

With no skin in the game, everything I make is straight bonus money. Keep in mind, that's just if I take out enough cash to cover what I put into the deal. The way I like to operate is to take out enough cash through refinancing to buy more property (creating more leverage).

If you thought that was exciting, we're just getting started. Up next is the first "E" in the C.R.E.A.T.E.™ Formula:

execution. Let's look at strategies for getting started in real estate.

GOLDEN EGGS

- Focus less on your income and more on building your net worth.
- If you think having a job is secure, change your mindset. Receiving a weekly paycheck ravaged by taxes is less secure than making hundreds of thousands or millions in real estate.
- Pensions and social security are not what they used to be. They are less secure and are shrinking as the years pass.
- Migrate from the left side of the Work Smart table to the right. Become a large business owner and/or an investor.
- The tax code benefits those on the right side of the Work Smart table.
- The R in the C.R.E.A.T.E.™ Formula stands for ROI (return on investment). Real estate offers a high ROI.
- The ROI in real estate includes cashflow, appreciation, equity buildup, and forced appreciation.
- Having more leverage (less cash in a deal) leads to a higher ROI. It also allows you to buy a bigger property or more properties.
- If you have zero cash of your own in a deal, your ROI is infinite.

CHAPTER SEVEN

BECOME A MILLIONAIRE

When I was a real estate agent, I worked with this guy named Peter. We both specialized in selling multi-residential property. I liked Peter, but he was lazy. He loved hanging with the guys and smoking cigarettes, and he'd do some work when he felt like it. His commissions were low, but so were his expenses, so he didn't care. He liked to take it easy and not work too hard.

One day, a client approached him about buying a thirty-unit building that was for sale. It was in a reasonable location and had mostly one- and two-bedroom apartments. The client asked Peter, "Why don't you throw your commission back into the deal and become my partner? You can move into the building and take care of it for me."

Peter accepted the offer. He got a percentage of the building and moved in, where he became the de facto janitor/ manager/building superintendent for the next few years.

A few years later, Peter's partner approached him and said, "I have an opportunity overseas, and I'm leaving the country. Would you be interested in taking my piece of the action?"

Again, Peter agreed. He financed the purchase of the property and became the sole owner of the thirty-unit property. He continued to live in one of the units and managed the building. The property became his life. He did nothing else but take care of it.

I moved on in my life and lost track of Peter. Years later, I was having breakfast at a restaurant, and there he was. He was sitting at a table with a leather jacket on, having a cup of coffee. I was surprised, because I hadn't seen him in so many years.

I went up to him and asked how he'd been, to which he replied he'd been doing great. When I asked what he'd been doing all these years, he told me, "I've been having fun. I bought a Harley. I'm riding across Canada, then down into the United States, just living the good life."

I was flabbergasted. Peter hated to work and only had that thirty-unit building. How was he living the good life?

"Remember that apartment building I bought a while back?" he asked me. "I became a millionaire from that building. I increased the rent and raised the net operating income. I refinanced it a couple of times and took some cash out. The income from the building covers my mortgage and my lifestyle. That's how I'm able to travel the world."

This conversation was an eye-opener for me. I thought, "This guy bought one building that's providing enough passive income for him to retire and drive cross-country on a Harley."

And it truly was passive income. Peter told me he hired a superintendent who takes care of the building. All Peter does now is cash the checks and oversee the superintendent. As lazy as he was, he made one smart move in his life, and it made him a millionaire.

My question to you is: is it really hard to become a millionaire?

No, it's not hard! Anybody can do it. I'll never understand why people think becoming a millionaire is such an impossible fantasy. Yes, I understand it's easy for me to say, given the success I've achieved. But guess what? I was in not-so-great shape when I jumped off the corporate track and decided to get into real estate investing.

Peter was by no means incompetent, but for as long as I've known him, he's never been a go-getter. What he had was the awareness and patience to become wealthy. Peter didn't become a millionaire right away. He held on to his building, and it paid off big time.

ONE BUILDING CAN CHANGE YOUR LIFE

You don't need to own 1,000 units or even one hundred units to become wealthy. As Peter's story shows us, a single thirty-unit property can put you on the path to wealth. I hope this fact fires you up like it did me. My hope is that you read Peter's story and think to yourself, "Shoot, I can do what he did. I won't stop at one, though. I'll buy twenty or thirty buildings!"

If Peter can do it, anybody can do it.

The fun part of investing in a piece of property is that it gives you options. Once you buy your first building, you can play the long game and hold the property for a couple decades. During that time, you can do what Peter did and fix it up, take care of it, reduce expenses, raise the rent, increase the income, and eventually pay off your mortgage.

At that point, the net income from your building is purely profit. In addition, property values always tend to rise over time. Your building is now worth far more than what you paid for it on top of your mortgage being paid off. It's the compounding effect in action, working to make you a millionaire.

If you've got a great property in an excellent location, holding it long-term can be a great play. Many wealthy people pass buildings down to their children when they die, instead of selling.

But what if you're more interested in short-term gains? We'll discuss the velocity of money later in this chapter, but let's look at an example that's the opposite of what Peter did.

Say you buy a thirty-unit building that's in rough shape but located in a good area. The rent is low, but you know you can get more. You structure the financing to leave yourself some wiggle room for repairs, which you undertake over the next three years.

You keep it simple: upgrade the flooring, maybe replace the windows and the furnaces, and add a fresh coat of paint throughout. You update the entrance so it's classy, not depressing. You add a new awning and give the building a name. Say the address is 1900, so you call it "Le 1900" or "The 1900."

Over time, you increase revenue as the units turn over

and you raise rent. Three years later, you have a beautiful building that you've named, cleaned up, improved, and given new life. Rents have gone up at least 20 percent. All these moves increase the perceived value of the building to tenants, mortgage companies, and buyers.

From there, you can revisit the mortgage company to refinance the property, giving you all your invested money back plus a few hundred thousand dollars more that you can use to buy another building or two. Or you can sell the building and use the profits to buy a bigger building where you repeat the process that just made you a fortune.

If you behave conservatively, you can acquire a bunch of properties with hundreds of units. If you want to be aggressive, you can accelerate things. I know guys in their thirties who began with a hundred units and are now up to almost 1,000 units. They know what they want, and they're going for it. I applaud their tenacity and single-minded focus.

The pace is up to you. You can move quickly, or you can move slowly. Both short-term and long-term paths are viable. It all depends on how you want to play things.

But how exciting is it to know that one building can make you a millionaire? Let's look at the recipe I used for buying my first building to see how you can do it, too.

THE BASICS

"How do I get started in real estate investing? What's the recipe for success?"

I get asked this question a lot, and most often it's because people don't think they have the financial resources to purchase property. My answer to them, as I've stated already, is that you don't need your own money. I like to use OPM (other people's money), which comes down to making connections, doing your homework, and negotiating well.

Let me give you an example, and then we'll dig into the details from there.

I find a property that I think is a good deal. After some analysis, I see that doing a few things to the building will cut down on expenses and raise revenue significantly. I make an offer and make sure I have a delay built in so I can find investors.

I take that property to people who have cash to invest. (It helps if I know them, but I don't necessarily have to.) I tell them, "I've negotiated a great deal on this property. Here are the numbers. It needs X number of dollars for repairs and updates. After two years, it will produce X amount of revenue (net operating income). I want you to put the money up. I'll take care of everything from A to Z. You'll get paid first out of the profits. I make nothing until you've been taken care of."

This is a magic formula I learned from one of Montreal's wealthiest real estate owners. You approach potential investors and say, "Here's an investment deal that I'm offering."

These deals can be sliced and diced several ways. For example, I could offer a guaranteed 5 percent return on half of the money they invest. The other half will go toward equity ownership in the building. An investor who knows you may be fine with that, or maybe you can do even better.

Or, they could reply, "Are you crazy? No way that you come in with no cash down and I get only that amount. Here's the deal: I put the cash up, but I want 70 percent of the property."

It makes sense: the investor is prepared to put the money up, so obviously they will want a preferential equity position and a guarantee that their money comes out first. Of course. Who cares?

You just negotiated 30 percent of a multi-residential property with no cash down. Anybody telling you it's impossible to buy a property without cash of your own is wrong.

When I started working with Norm, I didn't have a lot of cash, but I had a partner who believed in me. When we bought our first building, Norm was confident the deal would work, so he lent me my part of the cash down. I received my 50 percent of the property. Norm's only requirement was that I had to pay back his loan within five years. I actually paid him back in one.

You can use a hard-money lender, which is a real estate investor who makes loans that are secured by the real estate. They may demand an interest rate as high as 10 or 11 percent, but they can get you the cash you need quicker than a bank can and with less paperwork. You factor the high interest rate into the cost of acquiring the property and plan to pay off the loan (and its interest) in less than a couple years with income from the building or out of the proceeds of a refinancing.

Do you see the critical puzzle piece as we talk about working with investors, partners, and lenders when your funds are low? It's this: relationships are one of the keys to success.

If you're looking to utilize OPM, start by building a network of investors, people with lots of money looking for a good home to build on their wealth. You also need to network with real estate agents. Find out which agents are most active in your market and take them out for coffee.

Tell them that, even though you're just starting out, your plan is to acquire hundreds or even thousands of units. Let them know that if they work with you in the short run, they'll benefit in the long run. That's exactly what I did.

When I was starting out, I had some agents who supplied me a steady stream of properties because they believed in the vision and the plan that I had. That's a big part of building your network: making sure people believe in you. If you haven't done the work we've discussed so far in the book, that'll be more challenging. But if you've worked on your mindset, made goals, and acquired the knowledge you need, people will want to work with you.

You can also find property in other ways. Go down certain streets that you like and make note of addresses. Find the owners, and send them letters asking if they're willing to sell. They may not be, but maybe they own a different property they are willing to sell, or they might call you at a later date when they change their mind.

CRUNCH THE NUMBERS AND NEGOTIATE WELL

When you find properties you like, you'll need to crunch the numbers to ensure they make sense. (We'll touch on this here and then do a deep dive in the next chapter.)

Ask yourself: are the rents appropriate, or are they low?

How big are the units? Is this area rising in value? If I put X number of dollars down, can I purchase it?

My partner and I use a spreadsheet to analyze each property and determine if it's worth pursuing. For example, if we see a building where we can force appreciation and get a 30 percent initial overall return on our investment (ROI), we're likely to make an offer on it. The reason we look for a 30 percent return is to leave room for investors.

If you decide to move forward after running the numbers, the next step is making an offer and negotiating. This is a fine art and a learned skill. The first piece of advice I would offer is to avoid focusing on a single aspect of the deal, such as price. When you're purchasing real estate as an investment, there are many moving parts and price is only one of those parts.

My second piece of advice is to get creative. Imagine you're negotiating on a property you want to buy for $2 million. The seller is asking $2.5 million but will take $2.3 for it.

One option is to agree to that price, or close to it, but ask the seller for a vendor take-back mortgage, which means you as the buyer borrow funds from the seller to purchase the property. In this scenario, you could get 75 percent financing from the bank and maybe 15 percent from the seller, leaving you responsible for just 10 percent cash down. The remaining 10 percent could come from investors.

You're acquiring the property for a bit more than you wanted to pay, but you were able to get in there with some leverage and comfortable financing to be able to do some work on a property you know will increase in value. Not only that, the seller made it easy for you.

Here's another negotiating tip: tease out the other party's weakness.

If someone is selling a building for $2 million and you know they badly need cash, offer them a $1.6 million cash deal that will close in two weeks instead of two months. You might be able to acquire property for hundreds of thousands less than the original asking price or market value, simply because you fulfilled a need for cash the seller had. In this case, you will need to have investors and/or hard-money lenders lined up in advance.

Understanding your leverage in negotiations is always worthwhile. I like to listen when I go into a meeting, and if I have an agent, I give them a list of questions to ask: Why is the seller selling? What is the seller going to do with the proceeds? How did they come up with the price they're asking for the property?

Here is my take on when to speak at a meeting or during a negotiation. If you feel what you are about to say will have a positive impact on your meeting, then go ahead and say it. If you feel what you are about to say could have a negative impact or even a neutral impact, then don't say it. It's as simple as that!

The more information you have, the easier it is to develop a negotiation strategy.

EXPLORE DIFFERENT TYPES OF REAL ESTATE

I've talked a lot about multi-residential real estate in this book because that's my specialty, but there are other types of real estate out there worth checking out. For example, my most profitable deal was actually a student residence we sold for a $10 million profit. If you have a university in your city, student housing could be an excellent niche for you.

What I liked about student housing was challenging myself to think like a young person. What would I want from my residence while studying at university? I have friends whose portfolio of student residences is rapidly expanding because they get the highest price per square foot in their area while still creating layouts that students love. One thing they told me (that I noticed as well) is that students value a strong community orientation.

At one of their buildings, the rooms have this beautiful common space that is designed in a clean, classy American southwestern style. They also give students what they need: a washer and dryer, a kitchen, a desk, and private bedrooms. They've been so successful with this design that they don't advertise, because spaces are immediately filled through student referrals.

You can also make money buying semi-commercial property, where you might have a store downstairs and two residential units upstairs. Or you might buy a larger version with six stores downstairs and maybe thirty residential units upstairs.

I have a friend who deals solely with semi-commercial properties. The revenue for stores is much higher on a per-foot basis, plus he has a great eye for it, and he enjoys it. He will buy a property where the stores are lower-end but have great potential. He brings in the right kind of retailer, such as a Starbucks or Subway, which raises the value of the property immediately.

Another route might be strip shopping centers. You can either build a strip center or buy an existing one. You might have a group of low-end tenants with no anchor (AAA tenant), and you take the time to bring in an anchor pharmacy such as Walgreens or a bank, and then you can attract better retailers one by one. You can make a fortune doing that.

Another category is industrial property—large spaces rented for uses like manufacturing or other non-retail businesses. I do not work in this area, but I know several millionaires who do.

Some people get into self-storage. Some say that the market in self-storage is getting tougher and tougher, but my feeling is that there are different types of self-storage and that there is still room to make money in many corners of this market.

Of course, some real estate investors buy single-family homes. They clean them up, rent them, and use the income to continue acquiring more houses to rent. I would rather do the same thing on a larger scale with multi-residential buildings, but single-family homes could be a great place to start if you need to build up your funds for bigger investments.

You also have people who make money flipping properties, which means they fix them up and sell them within a year for a quick profit, in order to buy more properties or larger properties. Here are my feelings: if you compare the numbers over ten or twenty years between flipping and holding a property for the long run, you'll see that the long-term buyer usually does better with less work and exposure.

Some people involved in flipping hold certain properties for the long haul. They might be flipping because they need the income to buy a bigger property they may want to hold for the long run. Some people flip properties in order to work themselves into a large multi-residential property.

You can buy a four- or six-plex with large units and convert them to co-ops or condos, which you ultimately sell for large profits.

I know several people who are buying homes, small apartment buildings, or rundown hostels and repositioning them into Airbnb plays. They renovate the units beautifully and add technology to the mix. They end up with income many times higher than what the properties were originally producing. In fact, the cashflow can be immense.

If you want to explore this way of building wealth, be sure to study the zoning and conversion regulations/bylaws in your city. This is important, as many cities are now limiting the growth of this industry and restricting these properties to certain tourist areas. The bottom line is there's a ton of money to be made in this area of real estate.

How are you going to do it? I've given you some ideas. What are your ideas? Use the "magic page" I've included here to figure out which category of real estate speaks to you. There are no right or wrong answers. Get creative, and have some fun with this exercise!

HOW I WANT TO MAKE MONEY IN REAL ESTATE

....

....

....

....

....

....

....

....

....

....

UNDERSTANDING THE VELOCITY OF MONEY

When you're young, you can buy properties and hold them for decades. At my age, I'm more interested in the velocity of money, meaning faster returns and liquidity. When my partner and I first started, we did the financial analysis and clearly saw that holding for the long run, continually building the size of our portfolio, and managing the properties well offered the best route to wealth building and would make us a fortune. That's what we wanted to do.

But we both turned sixty recently (yikes!), and we did a bit of a reset and decided that it would be nice to make some money right now and have more fun. We saw people dying tragically in their fifties, sixties, and seventies, and it was a bit of a wake-up call for us both.

We took this new approach to our 160-unit property. It was divided between two concrete buildings of eighty units each with a swimming pool in between. We planned to renovate the buildings so we could raise the rent, decrease expenses, and increase the property's value. We used one of my favorite means of forced appreciation to help make this happen. (You'll learn more about how we did this in the next chapter—we created money like magic!)

We might put the property on the open market when the

time comes. We're confident an individual, a real estate trust, a public company, or even a pension plan will pay top dollar for two large concrete buildings that are fully rented and beautifully renovated.

If I was forty, I wouldn't even consider selling it. I would hold it, refinance, and buy more property.

Due to our age, Norm and I both mix in some high-velocity purchases with our long-term investments. In 2018, we sold three properties. One wasn't for us anymore and was becoming expensive to hold, one we sold for top dollar, and the other was the student residence, which we loved, but we felt confident we were getting peak value.

We have other properties that we have no plans to sell. Sometimes, it doesn't make sense from a taxation point of view to sell, either. You want to hold some properties long enough that you can depreciate the value and cover your income. We'll talk more about this in Chapter Nine—it's one of those strategies that make people think you're cheating the system! Of course, it's perfectly legal. You just need awareness to take advantage of the benefits available to you.

THE PARABOLIC EFFECT

At the outset, a property you buy may have low or no

cashflow. Also, the majority of your mortgage payments go toward paying interest. As time passes, certain things happen.

First, by increasing rents and streamlining expenses, your cashflow rises. As the years pass, the amount of capital paid through your mortgage payments (equity buildup) goes up. Your property will also appreciate. When taking all these factors into consideration over a long period, there will be a moment, usually after ten or fifteen years, where the ROI skyrockets parabolically. This is why most wealthy people keep their properties for the long run.

So, you can increase the value of your property substantially at the outset with forced appreciation, and the value also increases parabolically after ten or fifteen years. This raises an interesting question: at what point is it best to sell, if at all—early in the process, during or after the parabolic effect kicks in, or not at all?

I leave this in your capable hands, since all roads lead to greater wealth!

WORK HARD TO CREATE A LASTING LEGACY

A few years ago, I was driving from Montreal to Toronto with Norm and a friend named Richard. Like most big cities, Toronto has a lot of huge, high-rise apartment complexes. I pointed to one of them off the highway on the right and said, "Richard, do you realize that if you could figure out a way to buy that property right there, you'd be set for life? Not only that, your family would be set for life, and so would your grandchildren."

He snorted, as if to say, "Robert, you know I can't do that. It's too difficult." My mental response was, "Wait a minute. It's not hard to do; you just don't know how to do it."

Richard was an experienced property manager, so he could take care of any building, but in his mind, he had already put up a wall between himself and those properties. He looked at those high-rises and thought, "I can't do that," as opposed to "I'll figure out a way."

I asked Richard, "Is it hard to find a job, whether you're a kid fresh out of university or someone with twenty years of experience?" He said, "Yeah." I continued, "You'd better believe it. It's hard work to create a résumé, go out there and find a job, get an interview, and then go through that process again and again. If you are lucky enough to get the job, will you work hard every day and be shackled to your desk?"

Again, Richard agreed. I said, "Your employer is going to make you work a certain number of hours a day and days a week, and you'll be lucky at the beginning if you get two weeks of vacation a year. Your life will be structured, and you'll be taxed to the hilt. Freedom will be a pipe dream. Am I wrong?"

He said, "No, you're right."

"So, you're going to work hard all your life and spend time away from your children, versus spending some time and effort educating yourself. You can even do this part-time starting out, and while you might not get 100 percent of every deal, you can get 25 percent. As time passes, you'll be able to increase that amount by buying partners out. You can even structure deals so by the time you're finished, you're a 90 or 100 percent owner of that property."

Richard looked at me, realization dawning on his face, and said, "My God, you're right."

"That's just one property," I reminded him. "Once you're aware and you've got the first deal under your belt, you're going to want to do more deals like that. Maybe you'll end up opening a real estate trust and making yourself a few hundred million dollars."

Many people are like Richard. They see obstacles instead of opportunities. Their minds are filled with negative thoughts that hold them back: *That's not possible. I couldn't do that. I don't have the money; that's for rich people or for big companies. There's just no way I could pull something like that off.* The minute they believe these thoughts, they've fulfilled their destiny. They've actually shut themselves down from buying that property.

Here, I suggest the opposite to you. It is entirely doable and possible at any age. Educate yourself. Get out of the box you're in. If you get that one property, then you've just changed the destiny of your family's life by creating multigenerational wealth.

Multigenerational wealth starts somewhere. Many people are born into it, but others build a company like Apple or Facebook and create multigenerational wealth very quickly. I'm not saying that everybody can do this. Very few people can do it on that scale, but I'm pointing to real estate and saying that given some time, education, awareness, and execution, anybody can build multigenerational wealth if they really want to.

People like Richard will look at that building and think it's too hard to make it happen. Really? I would say that trying to get a job and working in a job is more difficult—and much riskier!

WHAT HAPPENS AFTER BUYING YOUR FIRST PROPERTY?

The first question people ask when they're considering real estate investing is "How do I get started?" After that first deal, the next question is always "What happens next?"

You need to have a plan for every property you acquire. Consider the velocity of money you want. Do you want to be like Peter and live off the income from one building? If so, you'll want to hold that building for the long term and work to slowly increase its value.

Are you trying to migrate from the left side of the Work Smart table to the right? If so, then you need to buy a second and third property, with the goal of eventually having a critical mass of properties or units that will move you over to that right side.

I have a friend doing exactly that right now. He's not leaving his corporate sales job until he has what he considers enough units to work for himself full time. I took the plunge because I knew I was going to be a multimillionaire and I wanted to work full time on it, but I understand that not everyone is that gung ho (or crazy). You should migrate to that right side of the Work Smart table when you feel you've got enough properties to do so.

When you get started, think of it as having Phase One and Phase Two goals.

When I started to buy property with Norm, our Phase One goal was seemingly aggressive. I wanted 500 units (or many more) in five years, but Norm wanted our goal to be 250 units (fifty per year). He needed the comfort of more conservative goals, so I agreed with the caveat. I said, "Norm, that's exactly what we're going to do, and we're going to do it easily." (I was exactly right.)

Phase One, year one, might start with buying one property and immersing yourself in learning management, but the Phase One, year two, goal is to have a few properties. It's important to ask yourself, "Realistically, how fast can I build this? How many units can I buy in a year?" Find a realistic but forward-thinking Phase One goal.

Your Phase Two goal might be to acquire another 200 units and retire. Or maybe you want to have 1,000 units in your portfolio and create a management company. You might want to open a real estate trust and go public with 3,000 or 4,000 units. Of course, this lofty goal will take much awareness, great contacts, serious execution, and time.

It depends entirely on you as an individual, where you want to go, and what you think is reasonable. Once you buy that first building, new goals will start coming to mind.

Whatever your ambitions, buying more property is a good goal. That's the "A" in the C.R.E.A.T.E.™ Formula and the focus of our next chapter: growing your assets.

GOLDEN EGGS

- A single thirty-unit apartment building can make you a millionaire over time.
- Take care of your baby, and it will take care of your future. Add an awning, give it a name, upgrade the entrances and hallways, and keep it clean. The tenants will pay for your mortgage and help you become wealthy.
- After you upgrade your building and raise the rents, you can refinance and take out all of your invested capital (and even more).
- Use OPM (other people's money). Find investors, partners, and alternative financing.
- As you start out in the business, offer favorable deals to investors. Once you have a proven track record, you can negotiate better deals for yourself.
- Learn the math. Understand the numbers. Negotiate well.
- Don't focus only on price. There are several ways to make a deal work. Try to get the owner to carry

a second mortgage (vendor take-back or balance of sale) in order to achieve more leverage.

- Explore different types of real estate, such as multi-residential, commercial, semi-commercial, shopping strips, industrial, student housing, senior housing, and more.

- Understand the velocity of money. You can invest for the long run and make millions, or you can plan on a shorter hold, upgrade the building quickly, and sell it for a faster profit.

- As the years pass, your building's return rises parabolically, especially after fifteen years.

- Instead of working hard to create a CV, post it, work with a recruiter, prepare for an interview (or many), and then work a minimum number of hours per day/per week/per year with limited vacation time, you can try to figure out how to buy a 200-unit high-rise and take care of your family (and grandchildren) for life.

CHAPTER EIGHT

GROW YOUR ASSETS

Let's start this chapter with a bit of magic, shall we?

No, I'm not talking about card tricks or pulling a rabbit out of a hat. I'm talking about something much cooler: using real estate to create money like magic.

In the previous chapter, I mentioned how Norm and I did this with our 160-unit property. Now I'll dig into the details and explain how we used a means of forced appreciation to increase the property's value by $1.7 million in a short time through a couple of simple decisions.

When we bought it, the property was not in great shape. It was in a blue-collar area, and the rents were very low. The two buildings needed some work. Yet we took the plunge while other investors stayed away, because we were able to see that property had a lot of juice.

One item we immediately looked at was the heating system. Before buying the property, we did our due diligence by inspecting the property, so we knew each building had three furnaces. They weren't that old, and most buyers wouldn't have messed with them, but we got several quotes for replacing the systems to make them as energy-efficient as possible. Montreal's winters are long and cold, so you want to optimize heating efficiency to keep costs low. After having a study done on the existing heating system, we were told we could save around $30,000 on our annual heating bill.

We decided to make the investment and replace the furnaces, which ended up costing just under $100,000 after we received some money through grants from the gas company and government incentives that are available to everyone. Let's see: we invested $100,000 and would receive a reduction of $30,000 in our annual expenses. That's a 30 percent return, right? Slam dunk, wouldn't you say?

Here's why those savings on our expenses are so important. Yes, we replaced the furnaces with more efficient ones, which was nice. But the $30,000 we would save every year also affected our property's value, thanks to the magic of net operating income (NOI) and capitalization rate (cap rate).

With a 5 percent cap rate (this rate depends on your city, the individual location, and the overall economy), we followed this simple formula: NOI divided by Cap Rate equals Value ($1 ÷ 5 percent = $20). In other words, for every dollar we increased our NOI, it increased our property's value by twenty dollars.

So that $30,000 savings actually represented a $600,000 increase in our property's value. Holy mackerel! Are you getting it?

If you put $100,000 in the bank, you might get 2 percent interest. Here we spent $100,000 on new furnaces, and because we saved $30,000 annually, we created $600,000 in value! So, that means we are receiving a 30 percent return via the direct savings and another $600,000 in increased wealth via the magic of increasing NOI.

If you did nothing else and wanted to refinance, the bank would give you 75 percent of that $600,000, so your $100,000 investment would put $450,000 in your pocket.

It gets better, though. A year after we installed the new

furnaces, we were shocked to see we actually saved $70,000 in heating costs, meaning our NOI rose by $70,000. You know what that means, right?

The value of our building increased by $1.4 million ($70,000 multiplied by twenty) using a 5 percent cap. I hope you're getting excited, because this is seriously crazy stuff.

Apart from changing the heating system, we also changed the insurance policy and saved another $15,000. This led to a $300,000 increase in our property's value without investing a penny.

That, my friends, is the magic of real estate. You can take any type of property and raise the NOI by fixing it up, raising income, and lowering expenses, thereby increasing your property value and multiplying your money four, five, or six times over. If you start looking at real estate like this, you'll see dollar signs in every building as you drive around.

It all comes down to creativity and the decisions you make, starting with what type of property to buy.

WHY I LIKE RESIDENTIAL REAL ESTATE

Real estate is a large category. It's everything from land

and residential property (anything people live in) to retail shopping malls, office buildings, industrial spaces, warehouse spaces, or small properties with stores. You can build a sparkling, brand-new building, or you can buy a rough, empty building that you clean up to attract new tenants.

There is money to be made in every category. I have friends who do extremely well in commercial and industrial real estate. That said, I chose multi-residential for a few reasons, starting with the fact it's lower risk. You can buy a commercial property with two tenants, and if one of those tenants leaves, you're now half empty. You're immediately exposed, and if you have a hard time renting, then you risk losing your property. It's simply easier to get a person to rent an apartment than it is to get a business to rent commercial space.

Let's say you own a thirty-unit building. If you have a vacancy, you're still collecting twenty-nine rents. If you have two vacancies, you're collecting twenty-eight rents. You can afford to be vacant for a while and survive—if not thrive—with such a building because vacancies aren't typically a long-term problem, lasting maybe a month or two.

Lower risk is important to me because I want to be able to sleep at night.

I also like residential because it's easier to understand. We all live somewhere, which means we know the basics of single-home or multi-residential dwellings. I also feel this is an industry that will always be relevant, if not growing annually. There is no more land being created, right?

Sure, there are things you need to learn when you're researching properties and starting to manage them, but this is not rocket science. It's a big part of the reason I wrote this book for young people: owning a building and managing it well is within reach for you!

This is not something that only adults get to do. By the time you get through reading this book, you'll have the foundation you need to become a property owner.

With residential property, the barrier to entry is low in terms of the knowledge you need to acquire and the cash you need to purchase property. You can totally do this!

OPTIONS WITHIN THE MULTI-RESIDENTIAL CATEGORY

Within multi-residential real estate, there are many niches you should consider. I've done a few of them. You could focus on student housing, which has become hot recently. Ten years ago, student housing had a negative stigma. There was a notion that if you put students in your property, they would wreck it and not pay their rent.

However, I always thought student housing was a great category, and when I ran the numbers, I saw it made sense financially, too. Due to the location near a university, the rent per square foot is usually higher on a student residence. Usually, the demand is higher than supply. If you think like a student (and their parents) and make the right decisions, you can make a fortune.

The friends I mentioned earlier in this niche love buying property that isn't yet student housing, such as a large house near the university. They retrofit the whole thing, adjusting the property so that it services the specific needs of students, and then they rent it (usually in advance). Those moves bring the value of the property up to two or three times the original price.

Another niche is senior living, which comprises two levels of senior care. There are senior residences with a high level of service (on-staff nursing, transportation for seniors, meal service, and more) and a more hands-off version for people sixty and over.

With the aging population in North America, this category will grow rapidly in the coming years. People in their sixties want to live with people in their own age group, not next to young people who play loud music and stay up late. They want to live in buildings created to suit their needs and that will deliver the services they want. To get a higher level of service, seniors are willing to pay a pretty penny (sometimes up to several thousand a month).

Then there are properties based on the community you're servicing, such as blue-collar workers near a factory. Truth be told, these are my favorite units to own.

Blue-collar workers have to live somewhere, and during economic downturns, they aren't likely to get laid off. Even if they are, they need a place to live and will still pay their rent. These units are always rented. You can't always say that about luxury units in big cities. When people have to step down from owning to renting during rough periods, they're typically not stepping down into luxury units. By the way, even those on welfare need a place to live and pay their rent.

On the flip side, if you buy a property in a white-hot area of the city center, you'll pay more for the building and might have negative cashflow for a few years. In the long run, you'll probably make more money, because you can charge more per square foot due to your location. Additionally, buyers are always ready to pay more (which means a lower cap rate) for a property situated closer to the city center.

There are pros and cons to each side of the blue-collar/white-collar discussion. I prefer blue-collar buildings because I have cashflow from day one, but there's money on both sides.

WHY YOU SHOULD BUY IN YOUR OWN BACKYARD

The key to buying real estate in any category is being an expert in your marketplace. You must learn your city or area and know it as well as you know your friends' names.

Which areas are experiencing growth? Where is the gentrification, meaning which areas are being renewed or seeing a resurgence? Here's one you might not think of: where are the subway stops? You can do very well buying property near subway stops, because people will pay more for a shorter commute to work.

I am a big proponent of buying in your own city. It's in your backyard, so you know the area. When you have problems with your properties, you can drive there, not fly.

Going into other cities opens a new can of worms. You have to depend on others to manage your properties, you need to learn what the market is all about, and you can get taken advantage of by insiders. I won't say that you can't make money doing that—you absolutely can—but it's riskier.

I know people who own property in five different cities and are doing very well. That's not the choice I made. I focus on Montreal (and surrounding areas). I know the market well, and I like this market.

As I said, you can certainly do well in other cities further away from where you live. I have friends who live in Montreal, but they own many properties in Toronto. They have made a tremendous amount of money in another city. Actually, I bought a couple of buildings in Toronto and ended up selling them after a couple of years. I did well, but I had partners managing them, and I depended on them to manage the properties efficiently. This was an area of constant friction during our partnership.

If you're starting out, set yourself up for success by spending the first few years working only in your area. If you live in a smaller city, you may make money there if you know it well, or you might buy in the nearest adjacent, larger city if you know that market.

When you become a market expert, you can develop a strategy that will make you your first million. We mentioned student housing earlier. If you have a university in your city that is experiencing an enrollment boom, with 40 percent of the students coming from out of town, you can seize that golden opportunity to provide them housing.

WHEN TO MANAGE YOUR OWN PROPERTIES

The ability to succeed in real estate is directly proportional to your ability to hold on to your properties physically and emotionally, which means you must manage them well. This is the secret sauce.

You want to manage your properties on your own when you're starting out. Not only will it save you money, you'll also learn the ins and outs of maintenance and keeping a building operational for tenants. Essentially, you're making bigger deposits in your bank account (no management fee) and your brain account (learning to manage property well).

You're going to deal with some stressful situations early on. That's just part of the process when you own real estate. I'll never forget a call I got from a tenant while we were having a New Year's Eve party. The weather was very cold, and a pipe had burst. I was having fun celebrating, and I complained to Norm because I didn't want to deal with the call.

He smiled and said, "You're framing this wrong. We're going to make millions with this property. It's the cost of becoming a millionaire. We'll do this early on, but later, we'll have other people dealing with it for us."

Norm was right. Managing your property is part of the game starting out.

The biggest help you can give yourself is developing a system for managing your property. Know who gets the call when a pipe bursts. Have a system in place that makes it easy to collect and deposit rent. Create an advertising plan so that units don't stay empty for long when you have a vacancy. Talk with an attorney about the eviction process in your city in order to cut down on headaches if that day comes (and it will). If you have a rental board in your city, get to know the rules. If you have good systems in place, it's easier to hold on for the long run, because your investment won't drive you crazy.

One of the friends I mentioned in a previous chapter who is working toward migrating to the right side of the Work Smart table and doing real estate part time is getting a crash course in managing his first property, an eight-plex. By taking care of it himself, he's learning to mind the numbers and handle his own accounting, which doesn't require an accounting degree—just a spreadsheet and some gumption.

I saw him recently, and the first thing he said was, "I need to find another building soon!" He's still working in his sales job, but he knew he'd never build wealth through his job. His strategy is to parallel his regular job with property acquisition. He bought one, and now he's looking for another one. Eventually, he'll have a few buildings, and then he'll step it up by bringing in a partner and buying bigger properties.

My friend is doing things the right way. He's hands-on right now because he wants to learn property management on this one building he owns. However, he doesn't want to do this work forever, and in that desire, I think we see an important lesson.

When it comes to property management, don't be a control freak.

When you acquire a critical mass of properties—meaning you can institute your own management team or outsource to a trusted outside management company—you will be able to spend more time working ON your business than IN it. You can still be hands-on, but you need people working for you so that you can work on buying more buildings. You can hire somebody to fix a broken pipe. You can't hire someone to find properties, evaluate them, raise money, and negotiate deals on the ones you like.

OUTSOURCING THE MANAGEMENT WORK

Before you hire a property management company or start

your own, consider hiring a building superintendent. A lot of the headaches associated with managing a building can be alleviated if you hire the right person to take care of it for you (like Peter did).

I've made many mistakes in the past by hiring the wrong people. My biggest piece of advice is to find someone you can trust and who is not a drinker. Maybe it's an older couple who's looking to downsize and wants to live in the building. Avoid problematic people, even if they can do the work required of a superintendent, because they'll inevitably create problems.

You can teach someone to unclog a sink. You can't teach someone to be trustworthy.

When Norm and I hit a critical mass of units, we chose to create a property management company instead of hiring one. We hired two excellent property managers and almost all the management work funnels through these people now. We use a reporting mechanism to keep track of the work they do, but we're relatively hands-off otherwise.

If you choose to hire an outside property management company, proceed with caution. Far too many management contracts are written in a way to promote counterincentive behaviors. They're structured to make more money when they spend more money, so they tend to be wasteful and incompetent.

Another problem is that bad companies can drive your property into the ground through mismanagement. One of the reasons you want to manage your properties starting out is to establish a baseline of how you take care of your babies, so to speak. That standard will let you know if the company you hired is doing an acceptable job.

Before you get to the point of signing a contract, get referrals from others in the industry and interview several companies. Here's a pro tip: ask to speak with tenants. They're the ones who deal with the property management company most frequently and have the inside scoop. If the tenants feel heard and taken care of, that's a positive sign.

There are definitely good property management companies out there that can provide an on-the-ground presence if you own property in another city. If you hit a critical mass of units and need the workload off your plate, property managers can be a blessing.

However, keep in mind no management company you hire will sit down and do an analysis of how you can raise your NOI. Their job is managing the property, not the business.

You can let go of the daily operations. Managing the numbers will always be your job.

THE NUMBERS YOU NEED TO KNOW

What numbers am I talking about, exactly? You've already seen a couple important ones mentioned at the top of this chapter: capitalization rate (cap rate) and net operating income (NOI).

Let's start with NOI. Look at the monthly revenue your property produces through rent, parking fees, laundry machines, storage fees, and more. Now consider your expenses: taxes, insurance, heating, maintenance (snow removal, landscaping, cleaning), vacancy rate, property management fees, and so on.

Subtract your monthly expenses from your revenue, and then multiply that amount by twelve (for the annual number). That's your NOI. (Keep in mind this is before any financing payments are considered.)

Remember what my dad said when I showed him my paycheck: "I don't care about your income. What did you make net?" The same principle applies here.

You can affect your NOI by raising revenue and/or decreasing expenses. You saw how Norm and I reduced expenses by changing the furnaces in our 160-unit property. Increasing your energy efficiency can pay huge dividends. You can even consider converting the heating to electric baseboard and having the tenants pay their own heat. As always, you must do the math carefully. Are the returns you will receive and the increase in value worth the investment?

You can also reduce your expenses by reducing your insurance premiums. We have a good relationship with an insurance company that works to save us money. For example, when we buy a building, the insurance cost is often too high. We bring in our insurance agent, and he might decrease the annual expense by up to $20,000, which is a huge deal because of the impact that savings has on the NOI and the property's value.

Don't neglect expenses that tie into maintaining your building. This is vital, as it affects the condition of your building as well as the perception of your tenants and any financial institution or potential buyer.

Cap rates vary from one city to the next and from one location within each city to the next. The national average for apartment buildings with larger units at this time is about 5 to 6 percent. Some large cities like New York, Chicago, and Toronto have much lower cap rates. If you're looking at buying a property, you can know the cap rate by dividing the NOI by the property value, whether that be asking price or offering price.

So, if you want to buy a property for $400,000 with an NOI of $20,000, what's the cap rate?

That's right, it's 5 percent.

Cap rate is important because it indicates economic risk, and most larger buyers look at the cap rate as their North Star. The lower the cap rate, the lower the perceived risk. You tend to see lower cap rates in big cities and higher rates in smaller cities and suburbs. Unlike big cities with more stable population trends and property demands in outlying areas, you don't know if property values will remain strong, which creates risk.

Ultimately, the market dictates the level of risk by pinning a cap rate to it. Big cities like New York and Toronto have cap rates between 2.5 and 4 percent. Mid-sized cities have cap rates between 4.5 and 7 percent, while smaller cities tend to be around 8 to 10 percent.

If you did the math, the cap rate would be much higher for businesses or companies than it is for real estate. The perception is that real estate is a safer, lower-risk investment than buying a business. Banks are usually willing to finance the majority of a property based on a low cap rate, which should send a clear message to you regarding real estate.

With a higher cap rate comes more cashflow. For example, if you had a 10 percent cap rate on that $400,000 building, your NOI would be $40,000. The reason it's riskier is because you don't know if you can sustain the rental rates and prices needed to maintain that kind of NOI.

That said, it's important not to obsess over cap rate. Pay more attention to the price per unit (and per square foot) and whether it's low or high for the area. Can you increase the property's value through certain decisions and renovations or by reducing expenses? This is where the juice is found.

Remember: when you change NOI, you change the property value!

When you know the cap rate of your area, it can help you in pricing your property if you want to sell. Just divide your NOI by the cap rate to determine the value.

For example, if your NOI is $50,000 and the cap rate in your market is 4 percent, the rough value of your property is $1.25 million ($50,000 divided by 0.04).

Does the magic formula I used earlier involving NOI and cap rate make more sense now?

When you increase revenue and/or decrease expenses, you increase NOI. For every one dollar you increase NOI, the increase to your property's value is equivalent to the NOI divided by the cap rate.

Using a 5 percent rate, we divide one dollar by 0.05 and get twenty dollars. For a 4 percent rate, it's twenty-five dollars.

Here we see another reason cap rate matters: in markets where the rate is higher, changes to your NOI matter less. When you divide one dollar by 0.08, for example, it's just $12.50. However, though higher cap rates have less of an impact, the magic still exists.

If you buy a building in a market with a 5 percent cap rate and increase the NOI by $2,400 in the first year, how much have you increased your property's value?

It's easy math: $2,400 divided by 0.05 equals a $48,000 increase in its value. How exciting is that?

With just ten units, increasing NOI that much is not difficult. It can be as simple as increasing the rent from each tenant by twenty dollars each month—that's nothing!

INCREASING REVENUE VERSUS DECREASING EXPENSES

Of all the numbers, NOI is king because it directly affects property value in a profound way.

With that said, your top priority should be to increase revenue and decrease expenses so that you can compound your efforts when it comes to increasing your NOI.

Raising rent is the most obvious way to increase revenue, but that potential can be capped if you're in an area with rent control or if you are already at market rent. Montreal, for example, is rent controlled (Régie du logement). There's a rental board, and if rents are increased too much, tenants can fight the landlord on it.

Even with rent control, there are many ways to generate more rent. You can renovate and upgrade apartments. You can split existing apartments into two units (more on this strategy in a moment). You can also take an existing unused space (maybe in the basement) and create new units from it. A building we purchased had a very large basement "party room" with windows. We received permission from the city, renovated the space, and added two apartments in this basement space. Our revenue and NOI increased, which, in turn, increased the value of the property in a short amount of time.

You can increase rent by improving the condition of the property. You can make cosmetic improvements, such as putting up an awning or enhancing lobbies and hallways. This will attract higher-quality tenants who will pay more.

If a tenant leaves and you have an empty apartment, you can repaint the unit, replace the carpet with real or laminate hardwood, and swap out the kitchen cabinet fixtures. You don't have to put a lot of money into these upgrades to increase the perceived value of the unit.

Don't be afraid to negotiate with your tenants. I do this all the time. I'll tell them I want to raise the rent by fifty dollars a month, but I'm willing to give them something in return: a new fridge, stove, or air-conditioning unit. You can have some fun negotiating with them.

A laundry room is an easy way to generate revenue. Even if the units have washer and dryer hookups, some tenants may prefer to save money by using your machines. Either put in your own coin-operated machines or outsource it to another company that takes a percentage of the revenue or charges a monthly fee. In either case, you can use smartcard technology that allows tenants to reload laundry cards with credit cards. Smartcards are more convenient for the tenants and make accounting easier for you. In our buildings that still use coin-operated machines, we have to count and roll the coins by hand!

You can do the same with parking. A building we bought had loads of free, outdoor parking in the rear of the building. It's our property, and there is no reason why the parking needs to be free. We decided to charge a reasonable amount, twenty-five dollars per month, and added exterior lighting and numbered spaces. We increased our NOI substantially without pissing off tenants.

If you pay for utilities like heat, you can increase NOI if you decrease the cost like we did by installing new high-efficiency furnaces at our large property. Replacing shabby, old windows with energy-efficient windows can also reduce heating costs (but do the math carefully), and there may be government grants available. You can also consider converting old central heating systems into electric baseboard heat, allowing you to shift the heating costs to the tenant. In this case, you will have to negotiate with the tenants to take on the heating expense. Remember, it's always about the numbers.

BUYING MY FIRST STUDENT RESIDENCE

Remember the student residence I mentioned earlier that Norm and I recently sold? I want to share with you now the full story of that property. I just love how it turned out and the fun we had creating a unique living space for students. If you're about to head off to college, I hope you're able to find a place as unique and fun as the one we created.

The student residence sat on land owned by a fast-growing, French-speaking CEGEP, which is the Québec equivalent of a junior college. The four-floor residence had 173 suites and approximately 241 beds.

The land was not freehold property; instead, it had an emphyteutic lease, which is particular to the province of Québec. It's a form of long-term lease that was an institution of Roman law (although derived from the Greek law) and found in civil and French law. In short, the building owner leases the land from, in this case, the CEGEP for a period of between sixty-six to ninety-nine years.

We owned the residence, but we leased the land the building sat on, meaning we would be required to pay annual rent to the college.

The owner was asking $7.5 million, and Norm didn't like the lease aspect, but the agent kept returning to us. I saw potential for it and kept the discussions alive. Over a period of eighteen months, and with rabid persistence and creativity, I was able to negotiate the original asking price down to $5.5 million. As we did our due diligence during the inspection period, I started noticing something very interesting about the residence.

Every unit included a desk, closet, bathroom, and kitchenette. However, 101 units were single rooms with one bed, while the other seventy-two had two beds, meaning some students would get very little privacy. I hated feeling so exposed when I was a student living in a dormitory, so I started to brainstorm ways to offer students more privacy. Construction codes and fire restrictions meant we couldn't put up walls randomly, but if we could think of other ways to offer privacy, then students would pay higher rent for those spaces.

We took thirty-two of the double rooms and built a five-foot wall between the two beds, then marginally raised the rent. In forty of the rooms, we installed a ceiling-high wall, added doors, and installed a new window on the side of the room that lost the window when the wall was erected. We were also forced to install additional ceiling sprinklers. In those units, we raised the rent significantly.

At the same time, we removed a couple of units to build a beautiful lounge with a pool table, 60-inch TV, and study area. We also found unused space and put in exercise equipment. Thinking like a student, we knew young people liked having areas to gather and work out.

Interestingly, when we asked our insurance agent to quote a new insurance policy, he noticed we had a building-wide sprinkler system. This lowered the previous insurance cost substantially.

We also knew parents and the administration wanted the students to be safe, so we installed ninety security cameras and a special secure-door system that utilized key fobs linked to each student and their unit, so we knew who was coming and going, and when. We enhanced the landscaping with the aid of the CEGEP and designated an area where bikes could be locked. We also created a superb interactive website and Facebook page.

Once we got the residence the way we wanted, I looked at statistics of students who stay in student residences on campus rather than off-site. The success rates of students on campus were much higher. Also, we were able to create an algorithm that showed numerically how students living in our residence saved money (and time), sometimes exceeding the monthly rent they paid. These facts helped us with our marketing.

I also developed a close relationship with the CEGEP, which helped with our rentals and allowed me to renegotiate the emphyteutic lease. I was even one of the honorary presidents of the CEGEP's charity foundation.

A short nine years after our purchase, and after several creative (even brilliant!) moves to increase the NOI, we decided to sell the residence for over $10 million in profit! I think that's a testament to listening to students, parents, and the administration about what they wanted from a student residence and being very creative and bold with increasing the NOI.

Sometimes, the best thing you can do for your property is admit that you don't know the best course of action. Let your customers tell you what they want. If you're open to learning, the market will educate you.

HOW LONG SHOULD YOU HOLD YOUR PROPERTIES?

As I stated earlier, one of the keys to success in real estate is holding on to your properties, which will test your emotional and financial control. It's important to negotiate your mortgages well so the finances don't pressure you. The reason you look for property management help when you reach a critical mass of units is to keep the emotional strain from wearing you down. You need to focus your attention on working on the business, not in it.

If you're young and these criteria are met, you should hold on to properties for the long run. When I give people that advice, their next question is usually "If I'm holding on to this property, then how am I supposed to buy bigger properties with more units?"

That's a good question with a simple answer: by refinancing your properties (more on that in a second) and bringing in outside investors, there's no limit to how much money you can bring in to expand your business and to acquire more property.

Holding is an especially good idea if you're in a prime location. Property in a good location will always do better than property in a mediocre location. You can still make money in a mediocre location, but an outstanding location—think downtown of a major city—has lower risk and better long-term value. These are the properties you hold.

I would consider selling (and have sold) when I can make a nice profit and have achieved much of the potential (juice). I would consider selling properties where the management is tough or time-consuming. But again, the question to ask before you sell is "What happens if I refinance this property?"

If you can pull some cash out and put it into another property (like in the United States) or put it in your pocket with deferred taxes (like in Canada), that's always a viable option.

When I started out, I silently hoped to acquire 1,000 units and never sell. Apart from a couple properties, we generally held. As I mentioned, only recently have Norm and

I decided to cash in some of our chips because we are getting older. We are still living off the golden eggs of the golden goose (which you'll read about momentarily), but going for a higher velocity of money has allowed us to put some money in our pockets.

For you older readers, you need to start looking at which properties you want to be part of your children's inheritance. Here in Canada, we have a horrible "death tax" that deems your properties sold when you die, meaning taxes are due. It's horrible because it penalizes those who have worked hard to build legacy wealth during their lives.

Not only does your family have to pay capital gains tax, they'll also pay the recapture on any depreciation you took on the property to protect yourself from taxes over the years (more on this in the next chapter). Footing this bill sometimes requires families to sell a property to get the needed funds, which can be complicated if the heirs don't deal with real estate. Sometimes, families sell properties for less than what they're worth, because they're under pressure from the government to pay taxes on the property.

Now, if your heirs are part of your business, that's another story. They'll have to pay those taxes (minus their ownership part), but they'll also know exactly what to do with the properties. These are questions you'll want to answer long before the issue of a deemed sale arises.

If you're a young person, your objective should be to acquire as much property as you can, build up your management skills, and take care of your "baby." As the years pass, that baby will become the golden goose that lays the golden eggs.

You might think I'm talking about one of Aesop's Fables here, and while the idea started there, it takes on a whole new meaning when applied to real estate investing.

LIVE OFF THE GOLDEN EGGS, NOT THE GOLDEN GOOSE

Young people like to spend money. I get it; I was young once. When I got that first paycheck, I felt like the richest man in Babylon. I wanted to go on a massive spending spree.

As a young person getting into real estate, this temptation is more dangerous, because the checks you're going to bring home will be bigger than any job you would get fresh out of university. That's why we're going to discuss the golden goose and its golden eggs. My hope is that it will change your thought process before you go out and blow all your money.

Your golden goose is your pool of assets. As a real estate investor, it's your portfolio of properties. The golden goose lays the golden eggs: relatively passive income that can cover all your monthly expenses and more. The bigger your golden goose (i.e., the more assets you have), and the more eggs your golden goose lays, the higher quality of life you can enjoy.

Robert Kiyosaki put it this way at a seminar I attended. He said he woke up one day and decided to buy a Ferrari. When he went home after a visit to the dealership and told his wife the exorbitant price, her response was brilliant: "Go buy an asset that will pay for the Ferrari."

If you want to know what it means to live off real estate, there's a perfect example.

Robert didn't sell a property to get the cash he needed. That would mean living off the golden goose, which is bad. He chose instead to buy an asset that would produce the income he needed to buy his dream car, meaning he was living off the golden eggs.

You shouldn't do anything to reduce the size of your goose. When you're young, you'll have a small goose that lays golden eggs here and there. Be patient. Make moves that grow your golden goose, because the aim is to live entirely off the golden eggs it produces.

Spending is always a choice. When you want something

that will bring joy to your life, like a new high-tech TV or a two-week vacation to Paris, remember that these purchases represent liabilities, not assets, because they're taking money out of your pocket. They also eat into your golden goose. I'm not saying you should save every penny, just that your golden goose should always be top of mind.

I think of all the dumb stuff I bought when I was young, and it makes my stomach turn. Had I started investing that money in real estate in my twenties, I'd be sitting with over $100 million right now due to the power of compounding over a longer time horizon.

There's no limit to the life you want to lead. You can do, buy, or see anything you want. But you must do it in such a way that you don't reduce the size of your golden goose.

USE REFINANCING TO YOUR ADVANTAGE

I've talked about refinancing a lot in this book, and if you're like me when I was younger, you're probably wondering, "How the hell does this work, exactly?"

Let's look at an example to see how refinancing can aid your wealth journey.

Let's say you buy a property for $1 million and have a

$750,000 mortgage. After three years, thanks to a higher NOI and appreciation, the property is worth $1.5 million.

When you go to the bank to get a new mortgage on the property, you can access 75 percent (or more) of that value, which is $1.125 million. Let's assume you've paid your original mortgage down to $700,000, leaving a difference of $425,000 between the new value and what you owe.

Congratulations—that's $425,000 you'll be getting as a check from the bank.

You didn't sell the property. You still own it, and it's still accruing value for you through increasing NOI, appreciation, and equity buildup (paying down your mortgage).

However, you just banked $375,000 in profit (plus the equity buildup) after putting up $250,000 of your own money three years earlier (perhaps more if you negotiated a lower down payment).

If you're in the United States, you'll want to use a 1031 Exchange to purchase another property with that money and avoid paying taxes. In Canada, you can pocket that cash if you want, though I recommend using all or most of it to buy another property.

Remember the story I shared in Chapter Five about refinancing our forty-seven-unit building and being handed a check for $300,000 each? I said then that I didn't spend that money wisely, and it's true. Rather than reinvesting my gains into another property and growing my golden goose, I paid off some debts and moved my family into a bigger house.

This is yet another opportunity for young readers to learn from my mistakes. Don't spend your golden eggs entirely on your lifestyle. Remember what Jay-Z rapped in "Diamonds from Sierra Leone (Remix)": "I'm not a businessman. I'm a business, man."

Think like a business when money comes your way. You're not rich just because you had a big payday. You're rich when you use that money to grow your golden goose.

I tell young people all the time: be smart with your money now and you'll never regret it. Think about the version of you thirty years in the future. That person is looking back through time at this crucial moment, begging you to make the right decision.

Don't make the same mistake I did. Make your future self happy, and play it smart.

TAXES KILL THE COMPOUNDING EFFECT

In this chapter, we've talked about ways to grow your assets, which is helped by the power of compounding. In the next chapter, we'll look at the "T" in the C.R.E.A.T.E.™ Formula and see how taxes kill the compounding effect, as well as ways you can sidestep the damage in the short term. Before we get into that discussion, allow me to remind you. You've seen how powerful compounding is: a single penny doubled over thirty-one days leads to over $10,737,000.

Isn't that crazy? A penny—a near useless piece of currency—turns into more than $10,737,000 within thirty-one days. I doubt even the math whizzes reading this could've predicted that outcome. Well, this powerful compounding effect can also be used in reverse. Yup, when a chunk of your compounding is taken by having to pay annual taxes, watch out!

To start the next chapter, you'll see what happens when you subtract 30 percent taxes from the total every day. If you thought this result was shocking, you ain't seen nothing yet!

That chart will help you understand why it's crucial to know the tax code and push it to the limit without breaking the law. You'll see why I said it's important to educate yourself and not rely entirely on an accountant, no matter how good they are (remember: it's not their money). The tax code is structured in such a way that it offers advantages. If you're willing to find the advantages that apply to you, it can save you thousands (if not millions).

If you want to keep from strangling that golden goose, read on.

The chart below shows you the power of compounding by doubling a penny for thirty-one days.

PENNY DOUBLING WITHOUT TAXES (31 DAYS)

Starting Capital: 0.01   Tax Rate: 0%

Compounding ROI: 100%   Number of Iterations: 31

		Without Taxation				
		Start	Profit	tax		net
Start	$ 0.01				$	0.01
1	$ 0.01	$ 0.01	$ 0.01	$ –	$	0.01
2	$ 0.02	$ 0.01	$ 0.01	$ –	$	0.02
3	$ 0.04	$ 0.02	$ 0.02	$ –	$	0.04
4	$ 0.08	$ 0.04	$ 0.04	$ –	$	0.08
5	$ 0.16	$ 0.08	$ 0.08	$ –	$	0.16
6	$ 0.32	$ 0.16	$ 0.16	$ –	$	0.32
7	$ 0.64	$ 0.32	$ 0.32	$ –	$	0.64
8	$ 1.28	$ 0.64	$ 0.64	$ –	$	1.28
9	$ 2.56	$ 1.28	$ 1.28	$ –	$	2.56
10	$ 5.12	$ 2.56	$ 2.56	$ –	$	5.12
11	$ 10.24	$ 5.12	$ 5.12	$ –	$	10.24
12	$ 20.48	$ 10.24	$ 10.24	$ –	$	20.48
13	$ 40.96	$ 20.48	$ 20.48	$ –	$	40.96
14	$ 81.92	$ 40.96	$ 40.96	$ –	$	81.92
15	$ 163.84	$ 81.92	$ 81.92	$ –	$	163.84
16	$ 327.68	$ 163.84	$ 163.84	$ –	$	327.68
17	$ 655.36	$ 327.68	$ 327.68	$ –	$	655.36
18	$ 1,310.72	$ 655.36	$ 655.36	$ –	$	1,310.72
19	$ 2,621.44	$ 1,310.72	$ 1,310.72	$ –	$	2,621.44
20	$ 5,242.88	$ 2,621.44	$ 2,621.44	$ –	$	5,242.88
21	$ 10,485.76	$ 5,242.88	$ 5,242.88	$ –	$	10,485.76
22	$ 20,971.52	$ 10,485.76	$ 10,485.76	$ –	$	20,971.52
23	$ 41,943.04	$ 20,971.52	$ 20,971.52	$ –	$	41,943.04
24	$ 83,886.08	$ 41,943.04	$ 41,943.04	$ –	$	83,886.08
25	$ 167,772.16	$ 83,886.08	$ 83,886.08	$ –	$	167,772.16
26	$ 335,544.32	$ 167,772.16	$ 167,772.16	$ –	$	335,544.32
27	$ 671,088.64	$ 335,544.32	$ 335,544.32	$ –	$	671,088.64
28	$ 1,342,177.28	$ 671,088.64	$ 671,088.64	$ –	$	1,342,177.28
29	$ 2,684,354.56	$ 1,342,177.28	$ 1,342,177.28	$ –	$	2,684,354.56
30	$ 5,368,709.12	$ 2,684,354.56	$ 2,684,354.56	$ –	$	5,368,709.12
31	$ 10,737,418.24	$ 5,368,709.12	$ 5,368,709.12	$ –	**$10,737,418.24**	

GOLDEN EGGS

- Acquire more assets in order to grow your golden goose.
- There is serious MAGIC in raising net operating income (NOI).
- NOI is the total income minus all expenses (before financing).
- Property value equals NOI divided by cap rate (capitalization rate). Raise NOI and the value of your property goes up by twenty-fold (and maybe more).
- Every time you raise the rents or lower expenses, you are creating wealth for yourself due to the profound multiplication effect.
- Multi-residential real estate is always in demand and offers lower risk. This category includes apartments, student housing, senior housing, and more.
- Start acquiring real estate in your own backyard. It's easier to control and manage; plus, you know it well.
- Create your own management company to take care of your baby as you grow.
- Outsourcing management is certainly an option, especially if your properties are in another city. But be vigilant. Outside management companies are often counter-incented.
- Know your NOI.
- Understand cap rates.
- Understand the price (or value) per unit as well as price per foot.

- Maintain your buildings well.
- Find new areas to create income, such as exterior parking, interior storage, extra apartments, transferring heating costs to tenants, and so on.
- If you are near a university, take a look at buying student residences, or converting houses or apartment buildings to student housing. You can get a much higher income per square foot. Think like a student and their parents.
- If you are young, I suggest holding on to your properties for the long run. Let the parabolic effect make you a fortune. You can certainly sell properties for quicker profit, especially if the property is hard to manage.
- Focus on growing your golden goose, not spending it! Live off the golden eggs. When you want to buy a Ferrari or go on an expensive vacation, buy an asset to pay for your new expense.
- Refinance your property to get your money invested out as well as extra capital you can use to buy another property.

CHAPTER NINE

PAY LESS IN TAXES

I hope you haven't eaten recently, because the chart I'm about to show you might make you want to puke. On the previous page, we saw the power of compounding illustrated as a penny that doubled every day for thirty-one days became over $10,737,000.

Now, I'm going to demonstrate the erosive power of taxes by showing you what happens when you shave 30 percent off the total every day for thirty-one days. It's not pretty...

PENNY DOUBLING WITH TAXES (31 DAYS)

Starting Capital: 0.01   Tax Rate: 30%
Compounding ROI: 100%   Number of Iterations: 31

Start	With Taxes	Taxed at the End of Each Iteration			
		Start	Profit	tax	net
Start	$ 0.01				$ 0.01
1	$ 0.01	$ 0.01	$ 0.01	$ (0.00)	$ 0.01
2	$ 0.02	$ 0.01	$ 0.01	$ (0.00)	$ 0.02
3	$ 0.04	$ 0.02	$ 0.02	$ (0.01)	$ 0.03
4	$ 0.08	$ 0.03	$ 0.03	$ (0.01)	$ 0.05
5	$ 0.16	$ 0.05	$ 0.05	$ (0.01)	$ 0.08
6	$ 0.32	$ 0.08	$ 0.08	$ (0.03)	$ 0.14
7	$ 0.64	$ 0.14	$ 0.14	$ (0.04)	$ 0.24
8	$ 1.28	$ 0.24	$ 0.24	$ (0.07)	$ 0.41
9	$ 2.56	$ 0.41	$ 0.41	$ (0.12)	$ 0.70
10	$ 5.12	$ 0.70	$ 0.70	$ (0.21)	$ 1.19
11	$ 10.24	$ 1.19	$ 1.19	$ (0.36)	$ 2.02
12	$ 20.48	$ 2.02	$ 2.02	$ (0.60)	$ 3.43
13	$ 40.96	$ 3.43	$ 3.43	$ (1.03)	$ 5.83
14	$ 81.92	$ 5.83	$ 5.83	$ (1.75)	$ 9.90
15	$ 163.84	$ 9.90	$ 9.90	$ (2.97)	$ 16.84
16	$ 327.68	$ 16.84	$ 16.84	$ (5.05)	$ 28.62
17	$ 655.36	$ 28.62	$ 28.62	$ (8.59)	$ 48.66
18	$ 1,310.72	$ 48.66	$ 48.66	$ (14.60)	$ 82.72
19	$ 2,621.44	$ 82.72	$ 82.72	$ (24.82)	$ 140.63
20	$ 5,242.88	$ 140.63	$ 140.63	$ (42.19)	$ 239.07
21	$ 10,485.76	$ 239.07	$ 239.07	$ (71.72)	$ 406.42
22	$ 20,971.52	$ 406.42	$ 406.42	$ (121.93)	$ 690.92
23	$ 41,943.04	$ 690.92	$ 690.92	$ (207.28)	$ 1,174.56
24	$ 83,886.08	$ 1,174.56	$ 1,174.56	$ (352.37)	$ 1,996.76
25	$ 167,772.16	$ 1,996.76	$ 1,996.76	$ (599.03)	$ 3,394.49
26	$ 335,544.32	$ 3,394.49	$ 3,394.49	$ (1,018.35)	$ 5,770.63
27	$ 671,088.64	$ 5,770.63	$ 5,770.63	$ (1,731.19)	$ 9,810.07
28	$ 1,342,177.28	$ 9,810.07	$ 9,810.07	$ (2,943.02)	$ 16,677.11
29	$ 2,684,354.56	$ 16,677.11	$ 16,677.11	$ (5,003.13)	$ 28,351.09
30	$ 5,368,709.12	$ 28,351.09	$ 28,351.09	$ (8,505.33)	$ 48,196.86
31	$ 10,737,418.24	$ 48,196.86	$ 48,196.86	$(14,459.06)	$ 81,934.66

Isn't that insane? Over ten million dollars is reduced to $81,935!

You need to understand that taxes don't just strangle your golden goose—they flatten it. If you don't have a strategy for negating their effect, you'll struggle to build real wealth.

I mentioned earlier that I didn't pay taxes when I got started in real estate. What Norm and I did was use depreciation (a strategy I'll explain later) to "cover" the income we made on our first property, the forty-seven-unit building, and avoid paying taxes the first year. We were able to put that money back into the building and raise our NOI significantly.

In this chapter, we're going to discuss some strategies I've used and others I'm familiar with that can help you avoid the erosive effect of taxes on your wealth. That said, I am not an accountant or a tax lawyer. You should always consult with professionals about the strategies you read here before you go out and start acquiring property. Not only are tax laws different between the United States and Canada, everyone's situation is also unique.

Let's start with a simple strategy for saving on your taxes: personal expenses.

DEDUCTIONS COME IN MANY SHAPES AND SIZES

One of the major benefits of being a business owner is that you get to deduct personal expenses that are business-related from your taxable income each year. As an employee, you get to deduct very few expenses, not nearly as many as business owners.

Think back to what we discussed earlier: the tax code was written in a way to benefit business owners, not employees. This is a perfect example.

When I first started in real estate, I struggled to get a handle on tracking and deducting my personal expenses that were work-related—for example, including my vehicle as a write-off since I used it to drive to my buildings, meet with agents, manage my properties, and more. Generally speaking, you can either take a mileage deduction on your taxes or depreciate your vehicle's value every year. Which strategy is the best choice for you really depends on how many miles you drive and what kind of car you have. In my case, I write off a percentage of my vehicle's lease payments as well as gas and repairs every year.

Depending on where you live, you can deduct other expenses, too. In my tax region, I can deduct a certain percentage of my home and utilities from my income since I work out of a home office. Other deductible office expenses include paper, pens, office supplies, office furniture, desks, bookcases, equipment, my computer—anything I buy for my office.

Also, a percentage (if not all) of all your communications can be deducted. This would include: landline phone, cell phone, internet connection, online meeting software, online file software, and more.

Entertainment can be deducted if you take a client out for dinner or drinks. As long as you discuss business—maybe there's a deal you're pitching an investor or broker—keep the receipt because that evening is tax-deductible.

My provincial government (Québec) tends to be unreasonable when it comes to certain items I believe are legitimate deductions. As you know, I'm a huge proponent of seminars and courses, especially those presented by great teachers like Tony Robbins and T. Harv Eker.

Every seminar I attend helps me grow my business, whether we're talking about the power of the mind or the best new ways to invest in multi-residential properties.

In my eyes, both types of conferences should be deductible because they're helping me grow as a businessperson, which, in turn, directly leads to the growth of my business. Yet I often find myself in an argument with the tax department, which doesn't want to allow these expenses. In my experience, governments are becoming more particular with this type of expense, especially if the event isn't local.

For example, I've gone to vacation locales like Fiji for seminars and was told I couldn't deduct that cost because, in the eyes of the government, I went on vacation and attended the seminar merely to deduct my travel costs. I understand why the government argued this way, but it's still frustrating when those trips are truly for business.

Don't be surprised if your government tries to dismiss costs like these as related to personal growth, not business growth. What's funny is that right after I undertook some "personal growth" by attending Peak Potentials Training with T. Harv Eker, my business growth skyrocketed. The government can assume there is no correlation, but it's wrong. Regardless, look for training and development that won't get flagged.

Depending on the tax structure you use to own your properties (an LLC versus owning them as an individual, for instance), you can also deduct business expenses related to your properties. Most small, regular maintenance costs come out of your expenses.

Replacing windows or a roof is an example of a capital expenditure. This type of expenditure is treated differently on your tax returns. When you do that, you essentially pay fifty cents on the dollar for the renovation and grow your golden goose partially off the back of the government.

THE MAGIC OF DEPRECIATION

Depreciation is a huge tax advantage for real estate investors. Put simply, depreciation is how the government acknowledges that an asset wears down over time.

Depreciation is unlike other expenses in that it's a paper loss, meaning you get to claim an expense without spending any money. The point of claiming depreciation as an expense is that you can offset taxable income and save money on your annual tax bill.

Let's look at an example that will help you understand how this all works.

Imagine that you buy a million-dollar property and the cashflow is $50,000 (assuming there is no financing). In Canada, you can claim up to 4 percent depreciation every year on a declining-balance basis. In the United States, you divide the property value by 27.5, which is the number of "useful years" a property has according to the Internal Revenue Service (IRS). How they got that number, I have no idea.

Taking a 4 percent deduction on the first year of a million-dollar building means you're claiming approximately a $40,000 loss of value the first year. (If you're curious, it would be a $36,363.63 deduction in the United States.) Just by claiming that one expense (that actually cost you zero), you've taken your taxable income from $50,000 down to $10,000. Paying taxes on $10,000 sounds a lot better, right?

The tax rate depends on your income bracket, but let's assume it's 25 percent. You'd owe $12,500 by not taking depreciation and just $2,500 if you did. When you're trying to increase the NOI of your building, an extra $10,000 in your quiver makes a huge difference.

This is what Norm and I did with our first building. We took the money we saved claiming depreciation and invested it back into our property, which raised our NOI.

It's important to note here the government is still going to get its money. When you claim depreciation, you're deferring taxes to the day you sell or die, whichever comes first.

If you want to sell the property used in the previous example twenty years after buying it, you're going to owe capital gains tax plus recapture, which is the amount you depreciated the property taxed at 25 percent (or more). In the United States, full-time investors can avoid paying these taxes with a 1031 Exchange, which allows you to trade one property for another.

Using depreciation to defer taxes to a later date gives you time to grow your golden goose and softens the tax blow early on when you're building your funds. When you sell, taxes aren't as harmful, since you've made significant money off the building.

That million-dollar building might be worth $4 million or $5 million when you go to sell it in twenty years through the magic of appreciation and equity buildup (since you'll have paid off the mortgage). When you first buy the building, you're depending on the cashflow, so that savings of $10,000 we saw earlier is crucial to you holding the building long-term.

When you go to sell your $5 million building, assuming you don't roll the money into another building, you're going to pay capital gains tax, the rate of which varies from zero to 20 percent, depending on your income bracket in the United States. In Canada, 50 percent of the profits you make from the sale are subject to the tax rate for your income level, which usually ends up at around 25 percent.

Maybe you owe $1 million for capital gains (a 20 percent rate) and $350,000 of recapture after claiming $1 million worth of depreciation over the past twenty years. Instead of walking away from the sale with $5 million, you pocket $3.65 million after taxes.

You're a multimillionaire now thanks to that building, which means you're more capable of paying that tax bill than you were before the property increased in value.

People are flabbergasted when they hear that I don't pay any taxes. They think I'm doing something illegal, but real estate allows this legal loophole. It's a bit of magic that smart investors use to their advantage, which means I want you to take advantage of it!

USE THE TAX CODE TO YOUR ADVANTAGE

The tax code contains advantages for you as a real estate investor, and you need to push it as far as you can within the bounds of the law. That's not just my advice; governments encourage you to familiarize yourself with the tax code and use it to your advantage.

Most of the investors in my circle of friends know very little about the tax code and ways to save on taxes. They source that work out to an accountant and let them handle everything. As we've discussed, totally offloading the tax-return burden is problematic for a few reasons.

Accountants can't afford to be as aggressive as you'd be, because you pay by the hour and they have other clients to assist, meaning they can't look through your situation to find every advantage possible. I'm not saying you shouldn't use an accountant. If they're skilled professionals, they'll provide invaluable assistance. What I am saying is that nobody will care about your money as much as you will, so don't flush it down the toilet by leaning entirely on your accountant.

This is true for any professional you hire to handle your money, be it a retirement planner or stock broker. The best chance you have to grow your money is to educate yourself.

There are so many more resources now to learn about the tax code than I had when I was young. Back then, we would have to read the tax code itself to understand it or talk with an accountant. Now you can read books, take an online course, watch a YouTube series, attend a local seminar, or take an accountant out to lunch and pick their brain.

Google is your friend. Do a search for "tax-free real estate investing," and check out all the wonderful blog posts and articles explaining tax benefits available to investors.

Search for questions you have, such as "Can I deduct

my mortgage interest?" Be specific with your country of residence.

You're not necessarily looking for mastery—just awareness. When you discuss your tax strategy with your accountant (which you should do multiple times per year), the goal is to have an educated conversation during which you contribute ideas, not just listen and nod.

If the idea of learning about taxes sounds mind-numbing to you, try incentivizing your efforts. If you manage to save money on your taxes, do something fun with the money: put it toward a vacation, buy a new pair of shoes, or put a down payment on a new Jaguar.

Of course, the best use of that money would be to grow your golden goose by purchasing another property or doing something to raise the NOI on a building you own, but as I've said previously, we have to leave room for fun with the money we make.

BUSINESS SAVVY + EMOTIONAL INTELLIGENCE

Up to this point, we've discussed the ways to build wealth through real estate, but it's also crucial for you to understand how real estate functions within the broader business landscape. To do that, you need emotional intelligence to go along with your real estate specific knowledge. People love to brag about IQ, or intelligence quotient, but your EQ (emotional quotient) is what will help you close deals in the business world.

People who have high emotional intelligence are usually described as being street smart or business savvy. What that means is people are naturally drawn to wanting to do business with them.

As we'll see, emotional intelligence—the second "E" in the C.R.E.A.T.E.™ Formula—helps you improve relationships and get the results you want in every walk of life.

Let's start that discussion by moving to the next chapter and kicking things off with one of my favorite stories in the book. When you read it, I think this concept will click for you.

GOLDEN EGGS

- Taxes destroy the compounding effect. Always look for ways to save on or defer taxes.
- Learn the tax code. Use it to your advantage. Pay less in taxes.
- Create a business that will allow you to deduct certain expenses, such as your car, home office, office supplies, business meals, and so on.
- Your building can be depreciated, leading to reduced

or no net income. This is a powerful tool to defer your taxes and catapult the compounding effect, so you can build your wealth quicker.

CHAPTER TEN

STOP FOLLOWING THE RULES

You don't need a degree from a prestigious university or letters next to your name (like MD or CFA) to become wealthy. Emotional intelligence, expanded awareness, and an adjusted mindset, along with a basic level of knowledge related to finance and real estate, will have a far bigger impact on your wealth-building journey.

Emotional intelligence is the secret ingredient to making meaningful connections in the world of business and closing big deals. It's not what you know or who you know—it's what you know about whom. The ability to relate to people and understand what they want at a deeper level will position you as someone with whom people want to do business.

If you don't like following rules, you'll be happy to know that a high EQ means you're no longer standing in line; you're finding a way to get to the front. Before you think I'm telling you to cut in line everywhere, let me share a story that explains what I mean.

Norm and I attended T. Harv Eker's Guerilla Business School a while back, and one night, the facilitator announced to the crowd of well over 1,000 people we were going to play a game. We would be divided into "companies" of four or five people and go around earning points (money) for our company by visiting tables set up around the auditorium.

As you can imagine, over 1,000 individuals and 250 companies competing to visit a handful of tables in just two hours seemed like a recipe for utter madness. I had no idea how the facilitator planned to pull this off with so many people in the room. I sat there looking around the room and saying to myself, "There's no way in hell this is going to work, especially in the given amount of time." I fully expected chaos to ensue.

The facilitator yelled, "Go!" Immediately, there were lines at each table one hundred to 200 people deep. I looked at those lines and thought, "I have to find another way."

As I stood back and observed everyone queued up at

tables, I asked myself if the facilitator said in his short list of rules that we had to stand in line. Nope, he never gave us that rule.

I decided to make a bold move. I went to the table nearest me, walked past the seemingly endless line, and snuck around behind the broker who was sitting there giving out points to people rolling dice one at a time. Without a word, I began massaging his shoulders.

People in line were staring at me like, "Who the hell is this guy skipping line?!" In fact, many started to shout at me, some even including profanities.

The broker turned around and told me, "OK, you're first in line," and he handed me dice. I rolled my dice, got the points (money) for my company, and practically skipped away from the table as the people left standing in line fumed behind me. They had seen what I just did to get my points without waiting and without breaking the rules of the game, yet not a single person moved.

Everyone stayed where they were in line, obeying some sort of nonexistent protocol. I guess they were afraid of losing their spot in line.

Meanwhile, I had already conquered another mile-long queue using my massage technique. I was headed to the third table when other people finally started to copy what I did.

However, the situation was evolving. With certain people aware of the shortcut, the massage technique was no longer working. I'd have to try something different at the next table.

As I approached the next table, I pulled out my wallet and handed the broker a twenty-dollar bill. No surprise: I walked away with my points before everyone waiting in line.

By now a few people were copying me, but 99 percent of the people kept waiting in line, watching but not moving. Their companies were suffering because they were stuck in a box of their own making.

At the next table, I offered the broker 1 percent of our company. Hey, why not? It was an imaginary company anyway. Once again, I got my points.

I saw the facilitator standing on stage and decided to have some fun with him. He wasn't an official broker who could give us points, but his rules didn't say he was unable to help grow our companies. I went up to the stage and gave him an elevator pitch of our company.

He was smiling like crazy the whole time. Finally, I asked

him, "If I give you 5 percent, will you give me $10 million?" He thought about it, then countered, "Give me 10 percent of the company, I'll give you $10 million." I then offered him 7.5 percent. He accepted the deal and shook my hand. He took out a piece of paper from his pocket, wrote "$10 million" on it, and said, "Here you go."

As I walked away from the stage, I looked around me at the mayhem. People still stood in the long lines, the majority never reaching the front of their first table.

I'm sure you know how this ended. Yup, our company won the game.

I want you to get out of whatever box you've put yourself in. The people who stood in line limited themselves and their ability to grow their business because they accepted roadblocks instead of looking for detours. They thought the point of the game was to stand in line until you got your points. They were wrong. The point of the game was to win.

By choosing to stand in line—even when they didn't have to—they lost the game.

We had a debriefing session at the end, and the facilitator reiterated that exact sentiment. As he explained, the game had two purposes: to exhibit human nature and made-up societal rules and to show us what was needed to successfully build our businesses in a competitive world. Most of us create our own rules and stand in line. This is certainly not the way to build wealth.

As in life, the skill needed to win the game was emotional intelligence. By understanding what the facilitator and brokers wanted and connecting with them, our company won the day.

NOT FOLLOWING ALL THE RULES IN BUSINESS

When you observe the business landscape around you, make note of which rules are legitimate and which are imagined. Which rules apply to you, and which ones are for those with limited means or awareness? When you begin to observe these differences and apply some creative thinking, you might find ways to work around imaginary rules, work with the legitimate rules, or make some new rules to obtain the results you want.

The game was an eye-opener for me. I didn't know what I was going to do when the game started. All I knew, instinctively, was that the landscape I saw didn't work for me.

Can you see how this same principle can apply to the business world?

Here's an example. Let's talk about banks for a moment. If you want to grow your wealth through real estate, you need to become friends with your local bankers.

That said, here's what usually happens. The lower-level bank employees are required to follow a set of rules given to them by their bosses. For instance, they can't extend credit in certain situations or offer a lower interest rate to an investor working on a deal. Because they're trying to climb the ranks at their workplace, they won't break those rules.

I don't blame these employees for following the rules they've been given, because there would be legitimate consequences to breaking them, like getting fired.

However, here's where I want to make a critical distinction: there are no rules saying you have to work with these lower-level employees. Nothing is keeping you from jumping up the ladder to work directly with the high-level managers who have fewer rules and therefore more flexibility to loan you more money or give you a better interest rate.

Standing in line usually gets you worse terms and less money, so don't do it!

Keep in mind, however, that this is not one of those times

where you ask to speak to the manager. Use a dose of emotional intelligence to achieve a far better result.

Call the manager of your local bank branch or even the regional office, and offer to take them out to lunch. If you're a young person, my guess is that they'll be impressed by your gumption and agree to meet with you. If you get the chance to meet, let them know your business goals and that you'd like to explore a partnership where you do most of your business with their bank.

This is not about trying to grease the skids, so to speak. You're merely articulating your desire for an ongoing partnership that could be beneficial to both parties. One thing is certain: you have bypassed the lower-level gatekeeper and can now get things done.

The same strategy is useful in other situations. Say you buy a building and want to change the zoning so you can build retail space on the first floor. You could do what's expected of developers and take your chances coming in cold before city council or the city clerk and pitching your rezoning plan. Or you could stop standing in line and develop a relationship with a councilperson who believes in your plan and will go to bat for you internally and at the meeting. You can certainly work with several councilpersons to achieve a consensus.

I do this in life and in business. When I'm at the airport check-in, after offering several pleasantries, I always ask to be given an upgrade, if it is at all possible. About a quarter of the time, I get bumped to business class free of charge. When I would visit a hotel with my girlfriend, I would tell the person working the front desk about our love story and, believe it or not, that has been enough to get us upgraded to a fancy suite.

I never cheat people, hurt people, or push in. I just find a better way to get things done.

CREATE A RIPPLE EFFECT WITH GENEROSITY

Emotional intelligence is about more than breaking down imaginary walls. It's also about treating people with a generosity that is contagious. As Tony Robbins explains, you can create a ripple effect when you do something wonderful for somebody else.

When I receive extraordinary service at a restaurant, I ask the waiter to bring out their manager. They get nervous, thinking that something is wrong. When the manager arrives, I proceed to tell them about the fantastic job the waiter did serving us. While the food was great, I explain, we'll return to this restaurant simply because of the outstanding service of this fantastic waiter.

"Take good care of this employee," I tell the manager. "They're a serious asset for you."

I've just made the server's day. Maybe the manager gives them a raise or assigns them better shifts moving forward. The manager also feels good knowing a customer is happy and that they hired a good employee. The waiter may go home and affect others with their excitement. Maybe their children, their wife or husband, their girlfriend or boyfriend, or their parents will be touched by the transformative ripple. The ripple effect moves outward from me to the server to the manager to their children to their friends—and keeps on going. You don't even know how many people can be positively affected by a generous gesture that costs you nothing except effort.

With tenants, you'll have fewer problems and have more luck making changes that increase your NOI if you treat them with love and respect. Embrace your tenants! Make a spreadsheet of birthdays, and send them birthday cards each year. At the very least, send every tenant an email on their birthday. Give each of them a small Christmas gift. Not only is this the right thing to do, it brings the law of reciprocity into play. When you do good things for your tenants, they feel the need to reciprocate by being the best tenant possible.

I mentioned meeting with bank managers and city

councilors earlier, but generosity can be used to build a relationship with anyone you want to meet. If there's a successful investor in your area, for example, and you want to meet them after attending one of their seminars, here's a strategy you can use. Instead of calling up their assistant and asking for a meeting, write that person a handwritten note explaining why you admire them. At the end, tell them about what you're trying to do and that you'd love to meet them.

Again, the point of using emotional intelligence is to build meaningful relationships, not manipulate people into doing what you want. The first reason I suggest writing a note is because if it comes from a genuine place, you're not being phony. Second, even if they don't meet with you, your generous gesture will be remembered. Should the two of you cross paths in the future, you've already laid some groundwork for a relationship.

TAKE TIME TO LISTEN AND LEARN

Here's another way to be generous. You can contact that same investor and tell them you're interviewing the most successful people in various fields in your city. If they'd agree to give you an hour of their time, you'll write a blog post or publish a podcast episode they can use for marketing purposes. You'll do all the work; all they have to do is talk with you.

What I've found is that successful people love to share their story and what they've learned along the way. They're proud of what they've accomplished, and if they're philanthropic at heart, they love the idea of helping a young up-and-comer like they once were. By asking to interview them, you're tapping into their desire to share and impressing them with your desire to learn. Again, this must be a genuine desire in order to avoid coming off as a schemer.

I have a friend who invites successful investors for a thirty-minute interview, which he records in his Tesla. It's like real estate carpool karaoke, à la James Corden. He posts these videos on his website and has received huge numbers of visitors and seen increased interest in his business.

Whatever time you have been granted with investors, bankers (or whomever), arrive on time or early! Punctuality sends a message that you respect other people's precious time. Come prepared, ask questions, and take notes. Most importantly, listen to what they say. I'm not talking about listening to ask more questions. I'm talking about generous listening, where you listen to learn and deeply understand. If you take that approach, you'll walk out with gold and perhaps a new relationship.

This is what smart people do: they listen and learn.

A word of caution I'll offer here is that you need to protect yourself from business advice given by people who are not successful. We all get advice from people around us, but when it comes to business, you must learn to weigh the advice you receive. Where is it coming from? Is it coming from a person who is poor and struggling or someone who seems to go from deal to deal without success? It might make that person feel better to throw out advice, but always take what they say with a grain of salt.

The best advice will come from people you respect because they've been in the trenches doing the work and succeeded. They have a verified track record of success. If they're a self-made success, even better. I respect anyone who builds wealth from ground zero.

Learn from people who have succeeded after making mistakes and bouncing back. They'll help you see pitfalls you need to avoid, because they might have fallen in themselves.

Whatever area you're seeking to grow in—marriage, parenting, personal development, business—find people who have been successful in that area, and ask them for advice. If you're going to make deposits into your brain account, make sure they're good ones.

Another word of caution: watch your ego when getting started in real estate.

Ego is not a bad thing. If you were to ask a major league baseball player, they'd tell you it takes a little ego to stand in the batter's box and hit a 100-mile-per-hour fastball.

An ego can help you accomplish great things. If left unchecked, it can also hold you back.

Many people feel the need to be right, which is counterproductive because it shuts them off from important information that could lead to their success. If you're new to a certain industry, be it real estate or otherwise, realize that you don't know what you don't know. Don't let your ego stifle your ability to learn, because you're afraid of admitting that you don't know everything. Listen to people who've found success and learn from them.

As T. Harv Eker likes to say, "You can be right, or you can be rich. You can't be both."

PERSISTENCE ALWAYS PAYS OFF

Persistence is a critical attribute no matter how you're trying to build wealth. The reason you keep working hard and making connections is that you never know when those two efforts will pay dividends in the form of a partner or investor saying yes to a deal.

There are countless success stories out there of famous

people who were told no over and over again, until finally, the door opened, and they got the yes they needed.

Jack Canfield and Mark Victor Hansen, the creators of the *Chicken Soup for the Soul* series, were supposedly rejected by 144 publishers before they found one who was willing to take a chance on them. Now there are 250 *Chicken Soup* titles that have sold more than 500 million copies in forty-seven languages. Had the creators stopped after one hundred rejections, that publishing empire would never have taken off.

Colonel Sanders of Kentucky Fried Chicken started at age sixty-five and was rejected 1,009 times before he found a taker for his chicken recipe. Now, there are over 20,000 KFC locations around the world, all because Sanders didn't give up.

One thousand and nine rejections. If someone told you no every day for almost three straight years, would you have kept going? That's what true persistence looks like!

Most people seem to quit after only one or two rejections. It's time to change this destructive habit. Don't take a no personally. It's just part of the journey toward success.

Several years ago, I went to a networking event. As I went from table to table, meeting different people and mingling for a few minutes, I came across an old classmate named Daniel. We caught up for a bit, and I learned that he was buying real estate in Toronto. He and his partners were about to buy a large property in Toronto and needed another partner, so Daniel asked if I would like to meet up and discuss the details.

Norm and I met with Daniel and his partners the very next day for coffee. They presented the deal, and we liked it. We shook hands and agreed to be his partner in buying a big concrete complex in Toronto.

To be part of the deal, the next step was securing extra financing, because we didn't have liquid cash on hand. We tried to refinance one of our properties that had equity built up, but the mortgage officer told us repeatedly, "No can do. Your mortgage is locked in for three years." Even the higher-level manager seemed resistant to our request.

We went to a different bank, told the representative the story, and asked if they could help us. Again, we were denied. We went to three other banks, and each one gave us the same response.

As we approached the fifth bank, our hopes of making something work were dwindling, but we remained resolute. As we made our case to the mortgage executive, he looked at the paperwork and was quiet for a moment.

Finally, he said, "We can make this work using a *pari passu* structure." This became another piece to our growth puzzle, since we had no idea this type of financing existed.

Basically, he offered us a second mortgage that blanketed the first. We got a great interest rate because there was equity built up in the property, and a few weeks later, we had the money we needed to make the Toronto deal work. That deal ended up making us a couple million dollars, but if we'd stopped after a few rejections, we'd have made zero.

I hope this chapter has shown you how powerful emotional intelligence is in all aspects of life, not just business. When you relate well to others, people will want to work with you.

This discussion wraps up the five aspects of the C.R.E.A.T.E.™ Formula. That said, I would never hand you such a powerful tool and not show you how to get started using it. In the next chapter, I'll show you some ways to get started building wealth right now.

GOLDEN EGGS

- Stop following made-up rules! Find shortcuts and better routes to achieve your goals.
- Don't stand in line with everyone else. There is always a side or backdoor entrance.

- Make someone around you feel good to create a ripple effect of positivity.
- Meet with and listen closely to successful people. What they can teach you is priceless.
- "You can be right, or you can be rich. You can't be both." —T. Harv Eker
- Persistence always pays off. Don't take "no" personally. It's just part of the journey toward success.

CHAPTER ELEVEN

CREATE WEALTH NOW

Now that you have the C.R.E.A.T.E.™ Formula in your back pocket, you are light years ahead of pretty much every other real estate investor. However, knowledge without action is just untapped potential. So in this chapter, we'll see some first steps you can take, including how to find a great partner and how to structure killer deals investors can't turn down.

But first, here's one more story that I hope inspires you to actually get started instead of sitting on the sidelines, waiting until you're "old enough" to go out and make a million dollars.

A few years back, Norm and I were looking at investing in Toronto. It's a tough market to get into because of the high demand and low cap rates, but also because the vendors are leery of buyers from other cities. One broker who was willing to work with us was a guy in his early twenties named Nathan. I flew to Toronto to meet with him, and he presented me a hundred-unit concrete building that I liked. I made an offer but didn't get the property, because multiple offers pushed the bid too high for our taste.

Despite not buying that building, I was impressed with Nathan. He was respectful, soft-spoken, and intelligent. He didn't BS me or try to sell me on the property when I came to visit him. Despite being in his early twenties, he seemed wise beyond his years.

What I liked the most, though, was that he kept in touch with me after presenting that first deal. He'd call me once every couple of weeks to check in and let me know he was working to find another property and would send it our way when he did. Sometimes he called just to ask how I was doing.

During one of our conversations, Nathan mentioned that he was exploring buying his own properties with partners. I was taken aback by how quickly he understood where wealth is built. It took me forty-seven years to get it right, and here was this young man in his twenties migrating to the right side of the Work Smart table at warp speed.

After a few months, Nathan called me and told me he

was putting together a group of investors (including some family members) through a limited partnership to buy a property in the Toronto area. By the time he made this call to me, Nathan had almost fulfilled his needs. But Nathan had promised me a chance to get in on his first deal, so he made room for another $200,000.

Based on my gut feeling about Nathan, I got in on the deal with a friend of mine and we each put in $100,000. Don't get me wrong: the deal looked good, too, but I so admired Nathan's loyalty, honesty, and his respect for the business that I couldn't say no.

Now that we've been working with Nathan for a while, I can also say I appreciate his thorough and timely reports. Nothing puts an investor's mind at ease more than good reporting. As an investor, when you do not receive reporting in a timely fashion, your imagination starts to run wild with worst-case scenarios. Regular reports give you tremendous confidence in the deal and the person who put it together.

I have confidence in Nathan and will absolutely look at deals he sends my way in the future. He's building up his portfolio and managing these properties himself. Can you do what Nathan has done? Absolutely you can. In the same way there's no expiry date on success, there's also no such thing as being "too young" to start building wealth. If you treat your investors with respect, learn all you can about the market in your area, and conduct your business honestly, the sky is the limit for what you can achieve.

HOW TO GET STARTED IF YOU'RE YOUNG

If you're young, how can you start taking meaningful steps forward?

If you're in high school or college, it's the perfect time to begin amassing the knowledge you'll need to succeed. Reading this book is a good start. Once you're finished, grab the books I put on the recommended reading list at the end of this book. They will help you further understand the concepts we've discussed, including those that relate to the mind.

Any time you want to make a splurge purchase, I want you to think about the story I shared from my younger days about the amount of money I wasted. Think of how much money you could earn if you put that money to work hard for you rather than feeding temporary gratification. Never forget it's about continually growing your golden goose.

Put aside at least 10 percent of your income so that when the day comes, you have enough for a down payment or at least part of one. You don't need a lot of cash to buy your first building, but if you're working with investors or partners, they may want to see that you have skin in the game.

Maybe you find a side hustle that creates income you can use for a down payment. I know young people who sell items on eBay and earn more than $50,000 a year. Start thinking along those lines. It's not just about your nine-to-five job but also your five-to-nine job.

Next, start getting a feel for real estate. Go online to find real estate meetings, networking events, and seminars. You should be able to find ones in your area or nearby that you can attend. Focus on multi-residential property, but don't limit yourself to that. Learn a bit about retail, about semi-commercial, about shopping centers, and about industrial real estate.

Attend networking events. Not only will you meet potential partners, you might also find a deal at one. It was through a networking event that I ended up buying property in Ontario that made us millions of dollars. I know it's a buzzword that makes some people roll their eyes, but I highly recommend networking. It's uplifting to spend time with people who have a great attitude and who are in growth mode. These are people with goals, energy, and aspiration. No matter what your age, choose to spend time with people like that.

Build relationships with the people you meet. You might even become accountability partners with some of them. Accountability is supportive and encouraging. Maybe you find someone who's starting out like you are, and you agree to hold each other accountable for the goal of buying one hundred units within the next year or two. It's good to have somebody who will push you, point out what's missing, and help you move to the next level.

Join mastermind groups, either locally or online. If you Google "real estate investor mastermind group," you'll find tons of great options that are affordable or even free.

Here's a cheap but powerful step I highly recommend you take immediately: get business cards printed. Vistaprint is one of my favorite companies to use. Make a simple, classy design with your contact information and the job title "Real Estate Investor." Keep cards with you everywhere you go.

When you meet somebody, hand them a card. They may not be your next partner, but they might know of a building that's for sale. I've made deals that way, when somebody I randomly met and gave a business card to referred me to somebody else.

Real estate is a social environment. You will meet a lot of people, so find a way to make yourself stand out from the crowd when somebody meets you. What can you say so that someone will remember you when you contact them in a week or in a year?

In my case, I decided that saying, "Hi, my name is Robert Luxenberg," was not enough to be remembered by people. Instead, I began saying, "Hi, my name's Robert Luxenberg, like the country. I'm a real estate investor. Somewhere in Europe, there's a castle with my name on it."

By introducing myself that way, I've created a connection in their minds that will help them remember my name. When I call them in a week, I'll say, "Hey, remember me? I'm Robert Luxenberg." They'll say, "You've got a castle in Europe with your name on it, right?" As silly as it is, that simple memory hack works like a charm. People remember me.

YOU DON'T NEED MONEY TO MAKE MONEY

The old myth continues to circulate that you need money to make money. As we've seen throughout the book, that simply isn't true. Yes, it helps to have skin in the game, but there are ways to buy property with little of your own money in the game—or even zero.

One reason to begin networking is that you'll meet

potential investors or business partners who can help you put a deal together. One thing I've learned is that people with money are always looking for a good return on their investment. Even if it requires them to put more cash into the deal, they'll do it if terms of the deal can be negotiated in a way to benefit them when the money comes out. Think back to the first deal I made with Norm.

I was just getting started and had little cash, yet when the time came to make the down payment on our first purchase, Norm lent me the money. Was it a good move on his part? Absolutely. Two things were at play: First, he was betting on me. He knew that I was the right guy—that I was honest, loyal, driven, capable, skilled, and hungry. Second, he knew he was not going to get to the next level with his investments by himself. He needed me, and I needed him. He lent me that money because he saw an opportunity that made sense.

When we refinanced that property and took cash out of the building, I repaid Norm immediately. We've been partners ever since.

Skin in the game gives people a level of comfort and security, be it an investor or partner. But if you find the right person, you can make deals without cash. Remember, a good deal inherently guarantees the investor's money. Don't let naysayers tell you what you can't do, and don't take no for an answer. There's a solution to everything.

You might not get 50 percent of the building if someone else fronts the cash, but what if you get 10 or 20 percent? When it comes time to refinance, you can use the cash you pull out of the building to buy out part of your partner's share, or even buy a new building.

This is a process that requires persistence and patience. Everyone's path in this game looks different. Don't judge your success by someone else's standard.

There's a company here in Montreal that owns some of the best real estate in the city. Over the past fifteen years, I've watched their signs go out in front of every decent building in every good location. I'd say they own well over 5,000 units in great locations.

I've met one of the founders, and his story perfectly illustrates this idea of persistence. Years ago, his partner tried to acquire some real estate during a bad economic period in Montreal. He made some mistakes and went bankrupt. He was sitting there with no credit whatsoever, but he had a vision of owning properties in great locations in the Montreal area and beyond.

He brought in some partners and told them, "I have a

plan, but you all will have to sign for me, because my credit is bad. I'm telling you, if you take a shot on this, I'm going to make you all hundreds of millions." He presented it well, and his business plan was sound, so one by one, investors began signing on.

The group proceeded to pick up building after building, all without the owner putting a nickel of his own money in at the beginning. Now, he's approaching billionaire status. He went from bankrupt to having a private jet and thousands of properties in Montreal and other big cities.

He has built legacy wealth starting from ground zero, and as his story shows, starting with no money and growing as an investor is achievable. I'm not saying you need to run out and buy 10,000 units. A purchase of thirty units can be a fantastic start, and if you're not interested in a high velocity of money (like Peter), it can be a great end.

PARTNERING WITH FAMILY MEMBERS

I know I'm blessed to have a partner as trustworthy as Norm. I also know that not everyone has experienced the same amount of luck I had in finding a business partner, so I want to share some insight now about what makes for a successful partnership.

Let's start with family members. If you have a good

relationship with your family, it's an option worth considering. I've had some struggles in this area, but I know people who got their start in real estate by borrowing money from their parents or their uncles.

My first piece of advice is this: you can't treat your family members like an ATM simply because you're related. This is a bad approach, and furthermore, it's disrespectful.

Treat family members like you would any other potential investor. Make a formal business presentation, and show them a plan that has all the components investors would expect: the building, the offer, the investor's return, the guarantees, and all the other details. They might be family, but you still need to give them a reason for putting up their money, and a level of comfort knowing what you will be doing with their money, and how it will be returned.

By doing so, you're saying, "I don't want you to invest just because we're family. I want you to invest because you're going to make money with me in this investment."

One of the secrets when you're pitching a deal to investors is to tell them, "Your money comes out first. You come before me. I don't make a nickel until you guys are taken care of."

I would do that with anybody you're pitching, but especially family.

The flip side of this coin is that you should expect your family to act like investors.

Some readers will be surprised and others validated when I suggest that you shouldn't necessarily trust your family in this regard. This doesn't mean they're bad people, just that they might be the wrong people to make your business partners. We've all heard horror stories of families torn apart over money, so I recommend a cautious approach.

There are certain characteristics you want to avoid, especially when it comes to family. Don't partner with someone who has a limited amount of savings to invest, because it will put pressure on the deal. Sometimes, deals take longer than you anticipate, or they're not exactly what you thought. You don't want to feel like you have someone looking over your shoulder every moment because their entire life savings is tied up in this one deal.

You want people in a deal who trust you and who will give you the time necessary to make it successful. The money someone puts into a deal needs to be money they can afford to lose and still survive. If losing that money will ruin their life, don't partner with them.

You also want people in a deal who aren't overinvolved and trying to micromanage your activities. This tends to happen with people who invest all the money they have, which is another reason to avoid people with shallow savings. These are the people who slow things down or overcomplicate every step of the process.

Your family might provide fertile ground for these less-than-ideal partners. Due to your familiarity with family members, one of them with little to no experience might try to overstep and tell you how to manage the property or where to invest the renovation funds.

Since long-term success comes from holding on to a property, and holding a property comes down to managing your emotions, you can see how this kind of setup is problematic.

Finally, if you decide to partner with family members, make sure they're supportive of your goals. This might seem like a small thing, but if you're starting out trying to build your confidence along with your portfolio, you don't need naysayers dragging you down.

THE MOST VALUABLE TRAIT A PARTNER CAN HAVE

No matter who your potential partner is, trust is what you're looking for most.

Norm and I have a system for evaluating people in this

regard. We put everybody on a graph at the zero point and then move them up or down depending on their actions.

When you meet new people, I recommend that you neither trust nor distrust them. Just start them at zero and go from there. Pay attention to their behavior when you first meet them, and notice whether their actions earn or lose your trust. Did they do or say something that irked you? On the flip side, did they do or say something that impressed you?

I believe first impressions tell you who a person is 90 percent of the time.

Norm and I use that as one of our rules, and it hasn't let us down. When we meet somebody, if they do or say something we don't like, we move on. If they do or say something that demonstrates they're honest, then we usually move forward with them.

We use this system because we want to insulate ourselves from people who will let us down. I don't think it's a good business practice to assume somebody who lets you down is going to change if you give them more chances. A second chance could cost you millions. It could cost you your reputation if you bet on the wrong person to turn things around.

Are there honest people out there who make a mistake at

the beginning but are worthwhile partners? Yes, but do you want to bet on finding that person? Watch someone's first move. In most cases, they'll show you who they are. Don't rush in and trust people from the outset. Let them earn your trust through what they say and how they act.

Be careful with people who exhibit feelings of entitlement and greed. This can be complicated, and it's something that I experienced. Someone may have lent you $10,000 and negotiated a 10 percent return. When you cash out for $500,000, that person may feel entitled to a bigger share even though you delivered on the agreed-upon deal.

You don't want to be in that kind of situation. The amount of money you make should not be relevant. You are only responsible to fulfill the deal that was fairly negotiated. Whoever your partner is, they need to understand that the terms of a negotiated deal are final.

Recognize if someone who is partnering with you, or lending you money, is the type of person who might make demands outside the original agreement. It might be family, friends, or complete strangers. They will have a reason—people looking to screw you over always do—but at the end of the day, you don't want reasons. You want honesty. You want somebody you can trust to honor a handshake deal, even if it's not written up yet.

That said, always get the agreed-upon deal in writing!

SEEK OUT COMPLEMENTARY PARTNERSHIPS

In a good partnership, one plus one does not equal two; it equals five or even more. When two people come together who are loyal and trust each other, have complementary skills, and possess the capacity to grow, they can become a stronger force as a duo than they would be flying solo.

That's what happened with Norm and me. Norm had several partnerships over the years, but none of them worked. In my case, I got into the game late and had never partnered with anyone before. We joined forces, and it worked. Does that mean we don't have arguments? Come on—of course we do. We have disagreements like you would with any other person. The difference is we don't let pride get in the way of resolving our conflicts.

We've been partners for a long time now. We've helped each other become wealthy, and we really trust each other. No matter what happens or what decisions lie in front of us, we're unified by our shared goal of building legacy wealth for our families.

If you're young, it's a great idea to find a partner around your age and grow with them as you build your real estate business. It's especially beneficial if you're both good at different things. For example, one of you is strong with sales, marketing, and negotiation, and the other is adept at handling numbers. Roles don't need to be set in stone, but if you can find someone who's good in areas where you're weak, it can be beneficial from the jump.

In addition to complementary skills, look for a partner who has goals similar to yours. If you're wanting to bust ass and build a real estate business in the next few years, maybe it's best you don't partner with someone like my friend, Peter. If I'd been interested in a higher velocity of money starting out, I might not have partnered with Norm, because he wanted to go a slower, more conservative route. Thankfully, there was enough overlap between our goals that it wasn't an issue. We aimed a little lower when we started working together.

TIPS FOR STRUCTURING CONTRACTS

Whether you're working with an investor or your partner, always be prepared when you present potential deals and investment opportunities. If someone came at you half-cocked and overconfident, would you feel good about doing a deal with that person? In my eyes, their poor preparation would make me question the validity of their deal.

When you're ready to make your pitch, keep in mind who

you're approaching and what their expectations will be. Sometimes, the other party will ask for nothing more than a weekly or monthly report. By sending that report, you're delivering them a feeling of comfort and security. Even if you have nothing to report, touch base anyway.

If you're too busy to send weekly reports but hoping to put a new investor's mind at ease, see if they'd be willing to accept monthly reports after the first year.

I had a bad experience in that regard. I made an investment and was supposed to receive monthly reports, but they never came. I had to beg for information that should have been freely and regularly offered. The experience ate away at my trust in the person, since the silence fed my negative suspicions. As humans, it's the way we're built psychologically.

As soon as I started getting monthly reports via emails and phone calls, I felt better about the deal. I just needed confirmation that the person I invested in was sincere, serious, and working hard. You have to manage people's emotions when working with them.

Also, if you keep everyone in the loop, you'll usually be given more room to work. The more you communicate, the stronger the relationship becomes with your investors and partners. As more trust builds, your investors will be less inclined to stand over your shoulder.

An exit strategy, or how you plan to cash out, is an important piece of any contract. Investors should know whether you plan to hold the property long-term or sell it quickly.

Along the same lines, include in your contracts a way to buy investors out at a certain point. It could be two years or ten years, but if they're making good money, most investors won't mind selling out if they're well compensated. The advantage of including a buyout clause is that when the property value starts to rise, you can grab a bigger chunk of the equity.

GET CREATIVE WHEN PAYING INVESTORS

At a seminar, I met a wonderful woman who had $200,000 (from an inheritance, I think), and she was interested in investing that cash into a deal Norm and I had.

We created a hybrid deal where we paid her interest on her money with postdated checks, which are checks meant to be cashed at a future date. She had thirty-six postdated checks (three years' worth) with the option to cash one each month. In my experience, postdated checks are comforting for investors, because it's like they already have their money.

The interest rate we paid was healthy, too. She would've gotten 1 percent from the bank. She got 7.2 percent from us, so she was thrilled with the return on her investment.

We also structured the deal so that she benefitted from equity (like a bonus), but if she took her investment out in the first ten years, she would lose some of that bonus.

The other thing we did was structure her payments as a return of capital, which created a tax advantage because she didn't have to pay monthly income tax when she cashed the checks. When she cashed out after ten years, it would be a capital gain.

She loved the tax solution, and it was a feature that we created. Not everybody does that. It's a great solution that we've used for deals with a few other investors.

Remember the rags-to-riches story I told earlier of the investor who went from bankruptcy to owning over 5,000 units in Canada's biggest cities? I invited his main partner to lunch recently to learn some tips for structuring deals. I loved one piece of advice he gave me so much that I have to share it here. It was an "aha" moment for me.

He suggested that when an investor puts money into a deal, say $100,000, you should have them put in $50,000 as a loan earning 5 percent interest. The other $50,000 would go in for equity, and the investor would get whatever the pro-rata share was for that $50,000 investment.

By using this approach, you get the cash you need without giving away $100,000 worth of equity. Our friend said investors like this kind of deal because they get to own some brick and mortar, but they also know their money is working for them by earning interest.

GOLDEN EGGS

- Put away 10 percent of your income to go toward wealth building.
- Join networking groups in your city and online.
- Build relationships in all areas of real estate or whatever endeavor you pursue.
- Create classy business cards. Give them out at every opportunity.
- You don't need money to make money. Use OPM (other people's money).
- When searching for a partner, you need honesty, loyalty, desire, and someone who complements your skillset.
- Your investors must always come before you. Be creative with how you reward your investors.

CONCLUSION

You possess the most powerful force in the universe: your mind.

They don't teach you how to use your mind in school. We have the ability to create the reality we want through the power of our mind, yet too many of us are held back by unfounded fear, self-limiting beliefs, and faulty money mindsets inherited from our parents.

Once you break free from the idea that you are your mind, you can use the powerful instrument between your ears to help you achieve your dreams.

By reading this book, you've started to lay a financial foundation that can serve as your springboard to success. As you move into the world of real estate investing and look to buy your first property, keep in mind the five components of the C.R.E.A.T.E.™ Formula:

Compounding: It is the compounding effect of money earning more money, which in turn earns more money, that will accelerate the process of wealth building for you.

Return on Investment: Real estate has several levels of return that make it easier to build wealth faster, especially when you understand and use leverage to your advantage.

Execution: A plan is just an idea in your mind until you execute on it. You can't get caught in a pattern of *ready, aim, ready, aim, ready, aim.* You must fire in order to make money.

Yes, you'll make mistakes along the way. That's part of the journey! Adjust and move forward. The path to success is not a straight line; it's a curvy, wild ride that goes up and down and up and down.

Don't let fear hold you back. When I first started, the thought of buying a $10 million building scared me to death. Now, I don't even look at smaller buildings, because my awareness and my capacity for success have grown too large to think small.

Assets: Your objective in real estate is to acquire assets that create enough passive income to cover your expenses and your lifestyle. It's the idea of growing the golden goose (your pool of assets) that lays the golden eggs (passive income). By living off the golden eggs instead of the golden goose, you're living out the definition of financial freedom.

I chose to specialize in multi-residential properties, but real estate is a broad category with endless potential. Do some creative brainstorming, and find a niche that sparks excitement deep within your soul. The process of building wealth should be fun, after all!

Taxes: Taxes cripple the compounding effect, which means you need to find ways to reduce their impact. You don't want to break any laws but rather push the tax code as far as it will go without breaking. Don't depend on an accountant. Do this work yourself.

Emotional Intelligence: People brag about their IQ, but EQ is what gets deals done in the world of business. The ability to build relationships and communicate in a way that gets what you want is one of the biggest advantages you can have as you start building wealth. Work on developing your emotional intelligence, and I promise it will pay big dividends for you.

MAKE THE MOST OF YOUR TIME

The reason I would trade my entire net worth for a young person's age is because time is the ultimate gift we've been given here on this earth. I can spend a million dollars and make it back with an investment, but once I spend my time, it's gone. There's no getting it back.

When I tell young people to start building wealth right now, it's about more than leveraging the magic combination of compounding and a longer time horizon. It's also about getting out of the habit we all have of wasting precious time. When you're young, you think you have all the time in the world and that you're going to live forever.

Let's look back at why both these mindsets are not only faulty, but downright dangerous.

Depending on where you live, the average lifespan differs, but let's assume for the sake of this discussion that it's eighty years, or 700,800 hours. Each day we live is made up of twenty-four hours, but since we sleep an average of seven and a half hours each night, we're only awake for sixteen and a half hours, leaving us 481,800 hours of life.

The average commuter spends up to two hours each day traveling to and from work. This figure knocks us down to fourteen and a half hours per day, or 423,400 hours of life.

When you factor in the time we spend in the shower and on the toilet, we're down to fourteen hours per day of life and 408,800 hours in our lifetimes.

According to Nielsen Media Research, the average American household watches four and a half hours of television per day, so now we're down to nine and a half hours of productive living, or 277,400 of lifetime hours. If you're wondering, that's just thirty-two years.

Yikes, we're running out of time! But it gets even worse.

About 85 percent of your thoughts are the same thoughts you had the day before—a replay of a time you already lived. Doesn't it make you wonder how many hours per day you actually have left to spend in the present? Based on the numbers we've crunched, most people barely spend an hour a day in the present moment, living life to its fullest.

Your real life span is much shorter than you think. It's not eighty years; it's not sixty years; it's not even forty years. Your life, in terms of productive, worthwhile living, may be as short as ten years total, or even less. This calculation does not consider the time lost to suffering from diseases or ailments, or the time lost by those who die prematurely.

Think about your life like a football game. The average

football game lasts three to four hours, but the official game is only one hour. On top of that, the average time the ball is in play is about eleven minutes. Your life is what happens when the ball is in play.

Stop and contemplate this for a few moments. I'm hoping that, like I did, you will stop your runaway train and think carefully about how you'll truly live the rest of your life.

WHAT ARE THE ODDS?

Here's another reason to start creating the life you want today: we're all lucky to be here in the first place. When you stop to think about it, our existence is a miracle.

I had this realization recently when I awoke from a vivid dream. It's a bit trippy, but I want to share that dream with you, because what I saw changed my perspective on life.

In the dream, I was journeying through the cosmos when I came upon a vortex of pure light and began to witness creation. All around me, the building blocks of a man were coming together. As helical strands of DNA raced about, I thought of the trillions of combinations of DNA that could have come together to make a life that had not been me.

Conception, life, birth—the improbability of it all danced

before me. How could a single spermatozoon struggle against 300 million competing cells, all wanting to be born into existence? I imagined that the race to life was like running the Boston Marathon against 20,000 participants. What an incredible feat it would be for one cell to beat out all the runners and win this prestigious event, I thought.

Then it hit me. In the race to life, I had run in a marathon 10,000 times bigger than the Boston Marathon. At the cellular level, where life begins, I had beaten the odds.

Among the fierce competition to find life, hundreds of millions of potential lives would never have a chance. But I did. In an explosion of life at the very moment of conception, two cells from my parents, a single possibility among millions, came together to make me.

Me! I won the impossible race!

I started to think about my great-grandparents, who gave birth to my grandparents, who gave birth to my parents, all with the same almost insurmountable odds of being born at just the right place and time to pass on the lineage that would become me.

Moving beyond my lineage, what are the odds of only one planet in an infinite universe having the perfect orbital distance around the ideal star, giving off just the right amount of heat and radiation? What are the chances that this planet would then have the perfect balance of elements and gases to create and sustain life?

I realized I was one in many billions or even trillions given the chance to experience life. I was no fluke! Nor was I just lucky to be born; I was blessed. I was selected out of trillions of combinations of genes and progenitor cells to bring my uniqueness to the world.

When I awoke, I realized I'd forgotten how precious life is, and in light of that precious gift we've been given, we shouldn't want to waste a moment of it.

As we wrap up our journey together, the empowering advice I offer you is to take control of your life before it's too late. Smell the roses. Cherish every fleeting moment with your loved ones. Do what you are passionate about. Start building your wealth and freedom NOW.

Spend as much time as possible in the present, where life resides. Find happiness and joy. Find your purpose and serve humankind. Do it now. Not tomorrow or next week...today!

If you're a young person, unshackle yourself from the expectations of others and chart the course for your life that makes you happy. If you're like I was—stuck in the corporate rat race and frustrated you're not financially free—take the next exit off the highway you've been on and use the lessons from this book to write a new ending to your story.

Years from now, when you're enjoying the life of your dreams, you'll be glad you did.

GOLDEN EGGS

- You possess the most powerful force in the universe: your mind.
- Every moment is precious and matters. Make them count.
- You are blessed to have been given life. Your chance was one in many trillions to make it here. Yup, you won the Boston Marathon to the power of a million.
- Start now!

APPENDIX

SOME BOOKS I RECOMMEND

- *Secrets of the Millionaire Mind*, T. Harv Eker
- *Think and Grow Rich*, Napoleon Hill (This is the bible of the mind; read the updated version.)
- *Rich Dad Poor Dad*, Robert Kiyosaki
- *The Richest Man in Babylon*, George Clason (I read this once a year and still find new insights.)
- *The Next Step to Waking up the Financial Genius Inside You*, Mark Haroldsen
- *Rich Dad's Cashflow Quadrant*, Robert Kiyosaki
- *The 7 Habits of Highly Effective People*, Stephen Covey
- *Outliers: The Story of Success*, Malcolm Gladwell
- *The Untethered Soul*, Michael Singer
- *The E-Myth Revisited*, Michael Gerber
- *How to Win Friends and Influence People*, Dale Carnegie

- *Mind Power into the 21st* Century, John Kehoe
- *The Instant Millionaire*, Mark Fisher
- *Speedwealth*, T. Harv Eker
- *The Power of Now*, Eckhart Tolle
- *As a Man Thinketh*, James Allen
- *Unshakeable*, Tony Robbins
- *Unlocking the Secrets*, Robert Luxenberg and Arnold Francis (OK, I know this is a bit of a cheat, but what kind of author would I be if I didn't recommend reading my other book?)
- *Good to Great*, Jim Collins

ACKNOWLEDGMENTS

My journey of change and growth began with the realization I was doing the same thing over and over again, expecting different results. Yup, the definition of insanity. I dug deep inside myself and concluded I had to take a leap of faith and find the answers outside my limited box. I read a plethora of fabulous books and attended a myriad of courses and seminars, which helped change my underlying mindset and my financial destiny.

I would like to acknowledge and thank the great masters and mentors who guided me through my transformation and taught me how to live an extraordinary life. From T. Harv Eker and Anthony Robbins to Robert Kiyosaki, John Kehoe, Napoleon Hill, and many, many others, thank you from the bottom of my heart.

A special thank you goes to my business partner and friend, Norm Gordon. We have been on an extraordinary journey of growth and success facing many challenges and experiencing many triumphs. Through it all, we have remained friends and loyal to each other's hopes and dreams. We have complemented each other's skillsets and learned from each other along the way. Honesty, loyalty, and commitment are the key factors that underpin a great partnership. We have all three and continue together still. Thank you, Norm, for your wisdom and insights, and thank you for your loyalty and brotherly love.

Finally, I would like to acknowledge my mother for all her love, support, and sincere belief in her oldest son. I love you, Mom. And to my three, children Evan, Sarah, and Deanna, I love you from the bottom of my heart and only want you to live extraordinary and happy lives. I hope my mentoring and this book will go a long way toward helping you achieve your goals and live the life you dream of.

ABOUT THE AUTHOR

As a young man, Robert Luxenberg did everything the right way. He was an honor roll student who sat in the front of the classroom and excelled in every subject. He was on the national swim team for Canada and broke several Canadian swimming records.

When he entered the business world, Robert continued to be a high achiever. He became a real estate agent after graduating from university and sold everything from industrial to multi-residential properties. While he brought home some big paychecks, he couldn't see what was right in front of his eyes: he was making investors millions of dollars through the magic of real estate, while he took home a commission that was fully taxable.

Frustrations mounted as Robert moved into the world of

corporate management as an executive, vice president, and senior vice president of several tech firms. He continued to over-deliver but was stuck waiting for his superiors to reward him for his efforts.

Everything changed when Robert stepped back to analyze his situation. He was a high achiever who had succeeded in every position he'd held. He was climbing the corporate ladder and on the verge of accepting a new position with a company to spearhead operations in the United States...yet he'd built zero wealth up to that point.

Robert decided it was time for a change. He rejected his new corporate job offer and partnered up with a real estate investor he'd worked with as an agent, to begin buying properties together.

At the same time, he began analyzing himself to determine how he operated. What he discovered through introspection, reading hundreds of books, and attending dozens of seminars was that his financial blueprint and beliefs about money weren't allowing him to become wealthy. Once he worked to remove those obstacles, he found the kind of wealth and success with real estate that he never would've found on the corporate fast-track.

Now, Robert is a multimillionaire investor with decades of experience in all areas of real estate: buying, selling, identifying properties, negotiating, managing, and financing. Pulling from the hard-fought lessons of his own journey, Robert came up with the C.R.E.A.T.E.™ Formula to show how wealth is created in real estate through compounding, return on investment, execution, assets, taxes, and emotional intelligence.

Robert has grown a beautiful portfolio since he started in real estate, and now, he wants to share what he's learned with a younger audience. He hopes to give them what he never had growing up: a signpost pointing to a path of unlimited wealth-building potential.

Mind, Money, and Wealth is Robert's third book. His first book was *The Third Q*, an award-winning murder-mystery novel he co-wrote with Arnold Francis about how the mind works to limit you and how you can get beyond that to create the reality you want. His second book, *Unlocking the Secrets*, was a nonfiction follow-up to his first. He again teamed up with Francis to deliver a synthesis of insights to help any person seeking success and happiness in their life make a brilliant new discovery.

Robert lives in Montreal, Canada, one of the largest and most cosmopolitan cities in North America. He has three beautiful kids: Evan, twenty; Sarah, nineteen; and Deanna, sixteen. Right now, they're all going through school, where none of them has been taught about their mind, the most powerful force in the universe, building real wealth, or the incredible opportunities within real estate.

As part of his legacy, Robert wants to leave his three children this book. It's a companion designed to help them understand their mind, how money works, and the ways to build wealth no matter what they choose to do with their lives and their careers.

Beyond his own children, Robert hopes *Mind, Money, and Wealth: What They Don't Teach in School* will be a gift to every young reader who dreams of becoming financially free and living life to the fullest.